Wicked wording

Reading SATs Practice

KS2

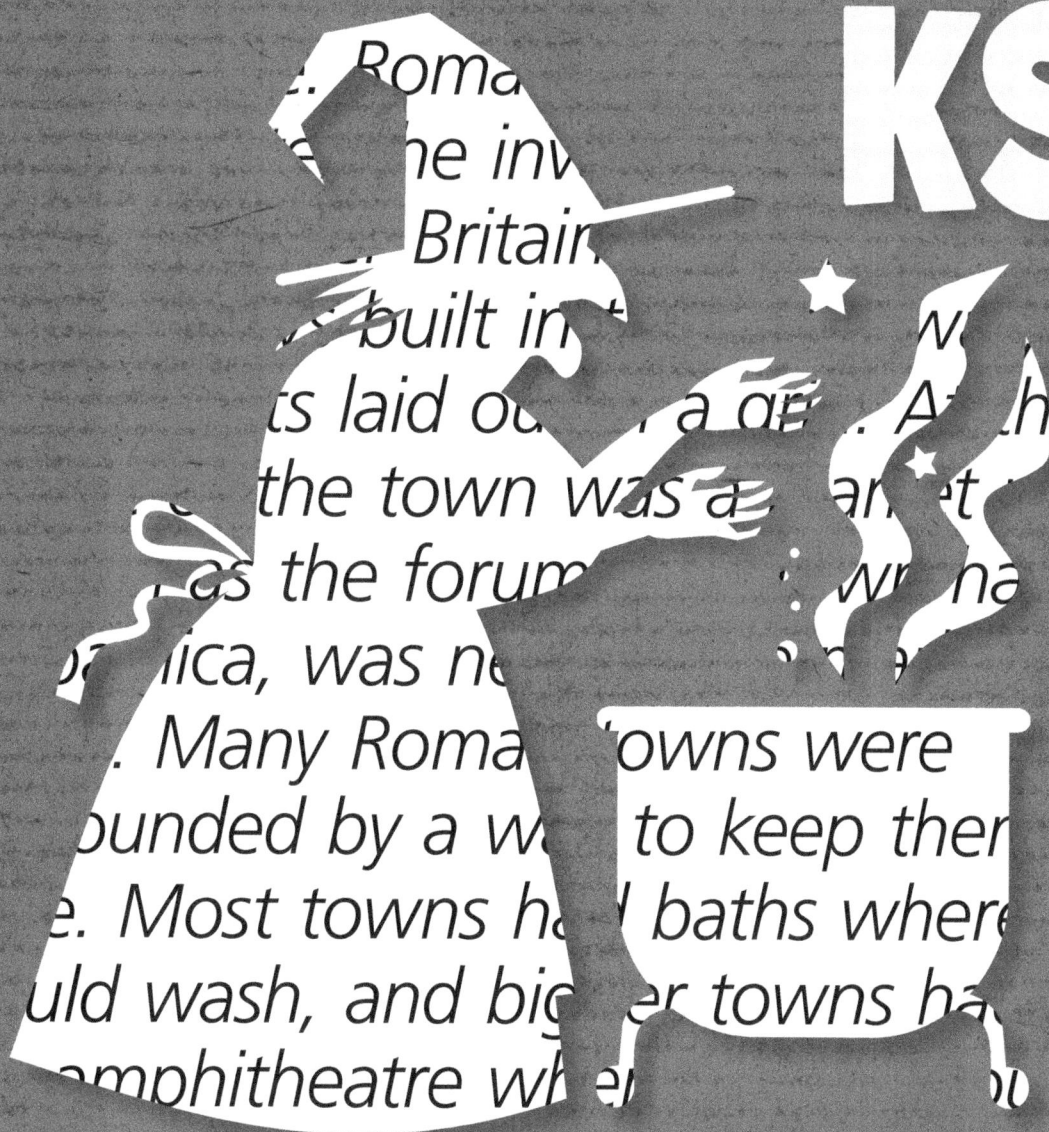

Rachel Clarke

About this book

Wicked Wording aims to help you teach pupils how to respond to the different types of questions included in the KS2 Reading SAT by providing varied practice of the language and question formats used in the national tests.

The book contains 15 units covering fiction, non-fiction and poetry. Each unit includes questions that build familiarity with the content domains that are tested in the KS2 Reading SAT. Each unit focuses on:

- *either* retrieval *or* inference skills
- *either* vocabulary *or* how words and phrases are used to enhance meaning
- *one from* summarising, predicting, identifying how content is related, or making comparisons across the text.

The questions in each unit build familiarity with the language used in the KS2 Reading SAT by closely modelling this language.

To reflect the three levels of text and questions found in the KS2 Reading SAT, the book is organised into three sections, indicated by 1, 2, or 3 stars. The categories are outlined in the Coverage Chart provided on page 4, which also indicates the content domain coverage of each unit, showing the number of questions per unit that relate to each domain. This means that the book can be used either consecutively or to practise targeted areas of the reading content domain, whether at whole-class, group or individual pupil level.

Wicked Wording and the reading content domain

	KS2 content domain reference
2a	give / explain the meaning of words in context
2b	retrieve and record information / identify key details from fiction and non-fiction
2c	summarise main ideas from more than one paragraph
2d	make inferences from the text / explain and justify inferences with evidence from the text
2e	predict what might happen from details stated and implied
2f	identify / explain how information / narrative content is related and contributes to meaning as a whole
2g	identify / explain how meaning is enhanced through choice of words and phrases
2h	make comparisons within the text

Analysis of the recent KS2 reading SATs shows that the majority of questions cover 2b and 2d. For this reason, each unit in this book is weighted toward one of these aspects of the reading content domain. This focus enables pupils to regularly encounter the language and visual structures used within these aspects of the content domain.

Question style

To help pupils gain greater familiarity with the language used in SATs questions, the book uses phrases from the national tests such as 'find and copy', 'according to the text', 'what impression' and 'what suggests'. The book also uses visual formats found in the tests such as multiple choice, join the boxes, and tick the true and false statements, again to build familiarity with the range of formats used in the SATs.

Teaching and assessing

Two teaching assessment pages are provided for each text. These contain an overview of the unit, advice for teaching aspects of the content domain, comprehensive answers, indication of the area of the content domain being tested and marks to be allocated.

Contents

Coverage chart

	2a	2b	2c	2d	2e	2f	2g	2h
*								
1. Echo and Narcissus	3			5	2			
2. Littlenose's Hibernation				8	1		1	
3. Fishbones Dreaming		6	3				1	
4. African spider bites banana shopper	2	6				2		
5. Roman Life in Britain	1	6						3
**								
6. The Happy Team	3			6	1			
7. Birthday Presents	2			6		2		
8. The Evacuee	2	6	2					
9. Swan Upping	2	6				2		
10. Christopher Columbus		6	2				2	
***								
11. A Person is Found	3			5				2
12. Midwinter's Eve	1			6		3		
13. The Apple-Raid	3		2	5				
14. Fantastic Mr Dahl		5					3	2
15. Greatest Ashes Moments	3		2	5				

Echo and Narcissus

All the goddesses liked to run through the silent woods on Mount Olympus, playing and chasing the deer. There was Queen Hera, soundless as the sun's rays; there was Diana, quiet as moonlight; there were the wood nymphs flitting like thistledown … and then there was Echo.

Echo was always chattering, arguing or shrieking with laughter. The deer scattered as soon as Echo opened her mouth.

"Echo!" said Hera sternly to her one day. "You've done it again!"

"What? Didn't do anything," said Echo pertly.

"Yes you did. You talked. You're always talking."

"I'm not!"

"You are. Don't tell me you're not."

"Not," said Echo, who always had to have the last word. "Not, not, not."

Hera was so angry that she pointed a magic finger at Echo. "Once and for all, be silent!"

The nymph was struck dumb. She put her hands to her throat, her fingers to her lips, and looked around in horror.

"Let this be a lesson to you. You always wanted the last word. Now you shall have nothing else!"

" … nothing else," said Echo. She found the words in her mouth, and they were the only ones she could speak.

"You may go now," said the queen of the gods.

" … go now," said Echo, without meaning to.

Echo ran sobbing off the mountain and wandered about miserably in the foothills. There, amid his flock of sheep, she saw a shepherd boy. He was combing his curly hair into ringlets and brushing the grass off his tunic. This was Narcissus, and Narcissus was as beautiful as any god. The shepherdesses could not lay eyes on him without falling in love.

Echo was no different from the shepherdesses. She fell in love with Narcissus at first sight, and what she would have given to be able to tell him so! But her lips were sealed like a locked door. All she could do was follow him about, her hands full of flowers and her eyes full of love.

"What can I do for you?" he asked, when he saw her gazing at him.

" … for you … for you," said Echo, and laid the flowers at his feet.

Unfortunately, Narcissus was quite used to women falling in love with him. It happened all the time. He knew how handsome he was and that made him very, very vain. Worse still, he did not much like women, did not want their sickly, syrupy love. Echo only annoyed him, trailing along behind him, saying nothing, staring with her mouth open.

"Everywhere I go, you follow," he complained.

from *The Orchard Book of Greek Myths* by Geraldine McCaughrean

Questions

1 *'"What? Didn't do anything," said Echo pertly.'*

Which phrase is closest in meaning to 'pertly' as it is used in this sentence?

Tick **one**.

Speaking cheekily ☐

Saying something prettily ☐

Speaking politely ☐

Not thinking about what you say ☐ [1 mark]

2 *'... the wood nymphs flitting like thistledown ...'*

What impression does this phrase give you of how the nymphs were moving?

.... [1 mark]

3 *'The nymph was struck dumb.'*

Which phrase is closest in meaning to 'struck dumb'?

Tick **one**.

Not very clever ☐

Hit on the head ☐

Sounding like a clock chime ☐

Unable to speak ☐ [1 mark]

4 *'... sealed like a locked door.'*

What does this description tell you about Echo's lips?

....

.... [1 mark]

6

5 'Echo ran sobbing off the mountain and wandered about miserably in the foothills.'

Why do you think Echo 'wandered about miserably in the foothills'?

....

....

[1 mark]

6 'The deer scattered as soon as Echo opened her mouth.'

What does this description tell you about how the deer were feeling?

.... *[1 mark]*

7 Write **two** things Narcissus did that suggest he was proud of his appearance.

1. ....

2. .... *[1 mark]*

8 'The shepherdesses could not lay eyes on him without falling in love.'

What is meant by the phrase 'lay eyes on'?

.... *[1 mark]*

9 '"Everywhere I go, you follow," he complained.'

Write what you think Echo would have said in reply.

.... *[1 mark]*

10 This extract is from a Greek myth. Using your knowledge of this type of story, do you think Echo will get her voice back? What makes you think this?

....

....

[Up to 2 marks]

Teaching assessment

The focus in this extract is on *2d make inferences from the text / explain and justify inferences with evidence from the text.* When answering questions about this text, pupils encounter the phrase 'what impression does this phrase give you?'. Being able to describe their impressions requires pupils to create an image or to visualise based upon what they have read. When encountering visualisation questions, you may find pupils benefit from drawing the scene or role-playing the actions being described. As is the case here, these questions often rely on pupils' understanding of vocabulary, so ensuring pupils are familiar with the vocabulary used in visualisation questions is vital.

Some questions about this extract ask pupils to identify the meaning of phrases as well as individual words. This is a part of *2a give / explain the meaning of words in context.* These questions allow pupils to explore some of the everyday phrases used in English, and to ensure that they understand their meaning.

(1) Speaking cheekily ✓

Saying something prettily ☐

Speaking politely ☐

Not thinking about what you say ☐ **1 mark** (Content Domain 2a)

(2) Pupils should explain that the nymphs were moving quickly and lightly.

Answering this question depends on pupils' understanding of 'flitting' and 'thistledown'. You may find it helpful to show pupils images of thistledown to support their understanding. **1 mark** (Content Domain 2d)

(3) Not very clever ☐

Hit on the head ☐

Sounding like a clock chime ☐

Unable to speak ✓ **1 mark** (Content Domain 2a)

(4) Pupils should explain that Echo's lips couldn't be opened, just like a locked door can't be opened. **1 mark** (Content Domain 2d)

(5) Pupils should infer that Echo was upset at this point of the story because she had been punished by the queen of the gods and she had lost the ability to speak.

1 mark (Content Domain 2d)

(6) Pupils should explain that the deer were frightened by Echo's noise.

1 mark (Content Domain 2d)

(7) Pupils should write 'he was combing his curly hair into ringlets' and 'brushing the grass off his tunic'.

This question asks pupils to understand that descriptions of actions often point toward personality characteristics. It is an example of the author showing rather than telling us about Narcissus's pride / vanity. **1 mark** (Content Domain 2d)

(8) Pupils should write 'see' or 'look at'. **1 mark** (Content Domain 2a)

(9) Pupils should write '… follow' or '… you follow'. **1 mark** (Content Domain 2e)

(10) Pupils should predict that Echo will not get her voice back. **1 mark**

Some pupils may be able to explain that the story is a myth and myths are used to explain natural phenomena. As this story explains the phenomenon of echoes it doesn't seem likely that Echo would have got her voice back if we have echoes now. **1 additional mark**

Up to 2 marks (Content Domain 2e)

Littlenose's Hibernation

It had been snowing all night; come to think of it, it had been snowing all *week*. The Ice Age landscape was covered in snow … and ice, of course. In the caves of the Neanderthal folk, snores came from under fur bedclothes, while the sun rose reluctantly over the trees, its pale winter light shining into the caves to tell people that it was time to get up.

Littlenose poked his berry-sized nose out of the covers, and quickly pulled it back again. He screwed up his eyes and shivered.

"If I had *my* way," he thought, "no one would get up at this time of the year. Everyone would stay in bed until spring." He pulled the covers closer around his ears, but only succeeded in letting in a cold draught.

The cold draught was nothing to the icy blast which hit him as Dad dragged the covers off. "Up you get," he shouted. "You can't lie there all day. There's work to be done. We're out of firewood, and Mum needs water from the river before she can make breakfast."

Pulling on his winter furs, Littlenose left the cave and trudged through the snow towards the river, a clay pot on his shoulder and a stone axe in his hand. "Fill that pot! Chop that wood! That's all I ever hear these days," he muttered to himself.

He muttered while he broke a hole in the river ice with the axe and filled the pot with water. He was still muttering as he brought it back to the cave, and he continued to mutter as he chopped a branch from a dead tree and dragged it home. "Stop muttering," said Mum. "I think you must have got out of bed on the wrong side this morning."

"If I had my way," thought Littlenose to himself, "I wouldn't have got out of *any* side of the bed at all."

Over breakfast, he continued to think: "People are stupid. Birds and animals have more sense. The elk left months ago for warmer places to spend the winter; and the wild geese flew away to the south where it is always summer."

The last course for breakfast was a few hazel nuts. Littlenose crouched close to the fire to eat them. "Squirrels eat nuts," he said to himself. "They collect them in the autumn and only get up to eat one or two, if they wake up feeling peckish. They sleep more or less all winter. I wish I could do the same."

Suddenly, he jumped up, scattering nuts all over the floor…

Littlenose's Hibernation by John Grant

Questions

1 *'It had been snowing all night; come to think of it, it had been snowing all week.'*

What does this description suggest about the appearance of the snow?

Tick **one.**

It was deep. ☐

It was white. ☐

It was melting. ☐

It looked fluffy. ☐ [1 mark]

2 Look at the second paragraph.

'Littlenose poked his berry-sized nose out of the covers, and quickly pulled it back again.'

Why does Littlenose do this?

Tick **one.**

He hurt his nose. ☐

He smelt something bad. ☐

He felt cold. ☐

He was hiding. ☐ [1 mark]

3 *'... he chopped a branch from a dead tree and dragged it home.'*

What impression does this phrase give you about the branch?

.... [1 mark]

4 Which of these words best describes Littlenose in this extract? Circle **one.**

grumpy   cheerful   mischievous   adventurous

Explain why you think this, referring to the text.

....

....

[Up to 2 marks]

(5) '… the sun rose reluctantly over the trees, its pale winter light shining into the caves to tell people that it was time to get up.'

What does this phrase suggest about the strength of the sun? Explain your answer.

....

....

[Up to 2 marks]

(6) Give an example from the text that suggests that Mum thinks Littlenose is in a bad mood.

.... *[1 mark]*

(7) 'The last course for breakfast was a few hazel nuts. Littlenose crouched close to the fire to eat them.'

Why do you think Littlenose crouched close to the fire?

.... *[1 mark]*

(8) '… Littlenose left the cave and trudged through the snow towards the river …'

What does this description suggest about how Littlenose moved through the snow?

.... *[1 mark]*

(9) Why did Littlenose need to break a hole in the ice?

.... *[1 mark]*

(10) What do you think Littlenose will do next? What makes you think this?

....

....

[Up to 2 marks]

Teaching assessment

The focus in this extract is on *2d make inferences from the text / explain and justify inferences with evidence from the text.* Questions about this extract have been structured to encourage pupils to give an opinion and then support it with evidence from the text.

This extract includes one question asking pupils to *predict what might happen from details stated and implied (2e).* In answering this question, pupils should be reminded to refer to what has been included in the text in order to make plausible predictions.

1 It was deep. ✓

It was white. ☐

It was melting. ☐

It looked fluffy. ☐   **1 mark** (Content Domain 2d)

2 He hurt his nose. ☐

He smelt something bad. ☐

He felt cold. ✓

He was hiding. ☐   **1 mark** (Content Domain 2d)

3 Pupils should explain that dragging the branch gives the impression that it was either too large or too heavy to carry.   **1 mark** (Content Domain 2d)

4 Pupils should circle 'grumpy'.   **1 mark**

Pupils should explain that Littlenose mutters throughout the text which gives the impression that he is grumpy. They may also refer to Mum thinking he must have got out of bed on the wrong side or to his view that 'people are stupid'.   **1 additional mark**

Up to 2 marks (Content Domain 2d)

(5) Pupils should explain that the description gives the impression that the sun was weak.

1 mark

Some pupils may explain how the use of 'pale winter light' indicates that the sunlight was weak.   **1 additional mark**

Up to 2 marks (Content Domain 2d)

(6) Pupils should write 'Mum suggests that Littlenose got out of bed on the wrong side'. Accept 'she tells him to stop muttering'.

Pupils need to understand the phrase 'to get out of bed on the wrong side' to answer this question.   **1 mark** (Content Domain 2d)

(7) Pupils should infer that Littlenose crouched close to the fire because he was cold.

You may want to activate pupils' knowledge and understanding of the world by talking about how they may have tried to keep warm near a fire on a cold day.

1 mark (Content Domain 2d)

(8) Pupils should explain that the phrase suggests that Littlenose walked slowly and with heavy steps.   **1 mark** (Content Domain 2g)

(9) Pupils should infer that Littlenose needed to break the ice in order to reach the water underneath.   **1 mark** (Content Domain 2d)

(10) Pupils should predict that Littlenose will try to hibernate.   **1 mark**

Some pupils may refer to the title of the extract 'Littlenose's Hibernation' and / or to phrases such as 'if I had *my* way … no one would get up at this time of the year' and how Littlenose feels that the animals have more sense than humans.   **1 additional mark**

Up to 2 marks (Content Domain 2e)

Fishbones Dreaming

Fishbones lay in the smelly bin.
He was a head, a backbone and a tail.
Soon the cats would be in for him.

He didn't like to be this way.
He shut his eyes and dreamed back.

Back to when he was fat, and hot on a plate.
Beside green beans, with lemon juice
squeezed on him. And a man with a knife
and fork raised, about to eat him.

He didn't like to be this way.
He shut his eyes and dreamed back.

Back to when he was frozen in the freezer.
With lamb cutlets and minced beef and prawns.
Three months he was in there.

He didn't like to be this way.
He shut his eyes and dreamed back.

Back to when he was squirming in a net,
with thousands of other fish, on the deck
of a boat. And the rain falling
wasn't wet enough to breathe in.

He didn't like to be this way.
He shut his eyes and dreamed back.

Back to when he was darting through the sea,
past crabs and jellyfish, and others
like himself. Or surfacing to jump for flies
and feel the sun on his face.

He liked to be this way.
He dreamed hard to try and stay there.

By Matthew Sweeney

Questions

1 Which of these options best describes Fishbones at the beginning of the poem?

Tick **one.**

a ghost ☐

a skeleton ☐

a cat ☐

a fisherman ☐ [1 mark]

2 What food was Fishbones served with when he was eaten?

.... [1 mark]

3 How long was Fishbones in the freezer?

.... [1 mark]

4 In the poem, how many dreams did Fishbones have?

.... [1 mark]

5 Find and copy the names of the other creatures in the sea with Fishbones.

.... [1 mark]

6 Using information from the poem, put a tick in the correct box to show whether each statement is **true** or **false**.

	True	False
Fishbones was unhappy in the bin.		
Fishbones was eaten by a man and woman.		
Fishbones used to jump out of the water to catch flies.		
Fishbones had lived in a river.		

[Up to 2 marks]

7 Number the following sentences from 1 to 5 to show the order in which they happened to Fishbones.

One has been done for you.

He lay in the bin. ☐

He was caught from the sea. ☐

He was swimming in the ocean. ☐

He was eaten. ☐

He was frozen. [3]　　　　　　　　　　　　*[1 mark]*

8 *'Back to when he was squirming in a net …'*

What does this description suggest about how the fish was feeling in this part of the poem?

.... *[1 mark]*

9 Which verse describes a time in Fishbones' life when he was happy?

.... *[1 mark]*

10 Which sentence below best describes what the poem is about?　　　Tick **one.**

A poem explaining that dead fish have feelings. ☐

The lifecycle of a fish. ☐

An explanation of why people shouldn't eat fish. ☐

A dead fish recalls events he's experienced. ☐　*[1 mark]*

Teaching assessment

The focus in this poem is on *2b retrieve and record information / identify key details from fiction and non-fiction.* When retrieving, recording and identifying key information from texts, pupils should be accustomed to questions covering a wide range of formats. The questions accompanying this poem include short answers, find and copy responses, indicating true and false statements and ticking to show the correct answer from a selection.

This extract also includes questions asking pupils to *summarise main ideas from more than one paragraph (2c).* You may find it helpful to encourage pupils to summarise the content of each verse of the poem in their own words. Some pupils may also benefit from putting events from the poem on a timeline so that they can appreciate that it is a story told in reverse order.

1 a ghost ☐

a skeleton ✓

a cat ☐

a fisherman ☐   **1 mark** (Content Domain 2b)

2 Pupils should write 'green beans and lemon juice'.   **1 mark** (Content Domain 2b)

3 Pupils should write 'three months'.   **1 mark** (Content Domain 2b)

4 Pupils should write 'four'.   **1 mark** (Content Domain 2b)

5 Pupils should write 'crabs, jellyfish and other fish like him'.   **1 mark** (Content Domain 2b)

6

	True	False
Fishbones was unhappy in the bin.	✓	
Fishbones was eaten by a man and woman.		✓
Fishbones used to jump out of the water to catch flies.	✓	
Fishbones had lived in a river.		✓

1 mark for **three** correct or **2 marks** for **all four** correct (Content Domain 2b)

7 He lay in the bin. `5`

He was caught from the sea. `2`

He was swimming in the ocean. `1`

He was eaten. `4`

He was frozen. `3`　　　　　**1 mark** (Content Domain 2c)

8 Pupils should explain that the fish was feeling uncomfortable as he was fighting for his life in this part of the poem.

You may want to discuss how squirming is a feeling associated with feeling uncomfortable.

1 mark (Contain Domain 2g)

9 Pupils should write that Fishbones was happy in verse 9.　　**1 mark** (Content Domain 2c)

10 A poem explaining that dead fish have feelings. ☐

The lifecycle of a fish. ☐

An explanation of why people shouldn't eat fish. ☐

A dead fish recalls events he's experienced. ☑　　**1 mark** (Content Domain 2c)

African spider bites banana shopper   *

Philip Travenen picked up a bunch of bananas at his local Sainsbury's supermarket and felt something prick his hand.

Glancing down he discovered a giant crab spider burying its fangs into his fingers.

The 65-year-old retired gardener collapsed in pain and was treated in hospital for 17 hours after the incident on Monday before being allowed home.

Sainsbury's yesterday apologised for the distress caused to Mr Travenen, who has emphysema, and delivered a free bag of shopping to his home in Newport, south Wales.

"He was distressed at being bitten," a spokeswoman for Sainsbury's said. "It is extremely unfortunate that this spider got through all our rigid controls and we apologise to the customer concerned."

The spider was taken to Royal Gwent hospital along with Mr Travenen. It was later sent on to Bristol Zoo where Warren Spencer, the head of invertebrates, identified it as a member of the family of giant crab spiders, or Sparassidae. Sainsbury's said the fruit had come from Cameroon.

"I picked up a couple of bananas and felt something sharp like a needle," Mr Travenen told BBC News yesterday. "It was the size of a 50p piece." He was worried he might die, he added, because he did not know the strength of the spider's venom.

Bristol Zoo said giant crab spiders were not particularly venomous. They are commonly known as banana spiders. The creature that travelled to Newport was dead by the time it arrived in Bristol.

In April a chef from Somerset used the camera in his mobile phone to snap a spider that had bitten him. It turned out to be a far more dangerous Brazilian wandering spider, (Phoneutria fera) which had also stowed away in a crate of bananas.

from *The Guardian* by Owen Bowcott

Questions

1 *'Glancing down he discovered a giant crab spider burying its fangs into his fingers.'*

Which word is closest in meaning to 'fangs'?

Circle **one**.

tentacles   tail   claws   antennae   teeth   *[1 mark]*

2 According to the text, how large was the spider that bit Mr Travenen?

.... *[1 mark]*

3 What is Warren Spencer's job?

.... *[1 mark]*

4 What happened to Mr Travenen as a result of the spider bite?

.... *[1 mark]*

5 Using information from the text, put a tick in the correct box to show whether each statement is **true** or **false**.

	True	False
Philip Travenen was a retired gardener.		
Sainsbury's gave Mr Travenen a free bag of shopping.		
Mr Travenen took a photo of the spider with his mobile phone.		
The spider was taken directly to Bristol Zoo.		

[Up to 2 marks]

6 Find and copy **two** other names given to giant crab spiders.

1. ....

2. ....   *[2 marks]*

7 Draw lines to match each extract to its purpose.

African spider bites banana shopper	Quotation
"He was distressed at being bitten."	Headline

[1 mark]

8 '… which had also stowed away in a crate of bananas.'

Which phrase is closest in meaning to 'stowed away'?

Tick **one.**

Hide away to make a secret journey ☐

Get lost ☐

Eat bananas ☐

Hide away from predators ☐

Hibernate ☐ [1 mark]

9 'Sainsbury's said the fruit had come from Cameroon.'

Find and copy another phrase from the text that refers to the origins of the spider.

.... [1 mark]

10 According to the text, which of the two spiders mentioned is more poisonous?

.... [1 mark]

Teaching assessment

The focus in this extract is on *2b retrieve and record information / identify key details from fiction and non-fiction*. Phrases such as 'find and copy' and 'according to the text' are used in questions about this text to remind pupils to refer to what they have read and to use this evidence in their responses. To answer some questions about this text, pupils need to read across the text to connect information.

This extract also includes questions asking pupils to *identify / explain how information / narrative content is related and contributes to meaning as a whole (2f)* by answering questions where they identify narrative content such as headings and titles.

(1) Pupils should circle 'teeth'. **1 mark** (Content Domain 2a)

(2) Pupils should write 'It was the size of a 50p piece'. **1 mark** (Content Domain 2b)

(3) Pupils should write 'head of invertebrates / head of invertebrates at Bristol Zoo'.

1 mark (Content Domain 2b)

(4) Pupils should write that Mr Travenen collapsed in pain and needed to attend hospital.

1 mark (Content Domain 2b)

(5)

	True	False
Philip Travenen was a retired gardener.	✓	
Sainsbury's gave Mr Travenen a free bag of shopping.	✓	
Mr Travenen took a photo of the spider with his mobile phone.		✓
The spider was taken directly to Bristol Zoo.		✓

1 mark for **three** correct or **2 marks** for **all four** correct (Content Domain 2b)

(6) Pupils should write 'banana spider' and 'Sparassidae'.

Pupils need to read across the text to locate both parts of this answer.

Award **1 mark** for each correct answer up to **2 marks** (Content Domain 2b)

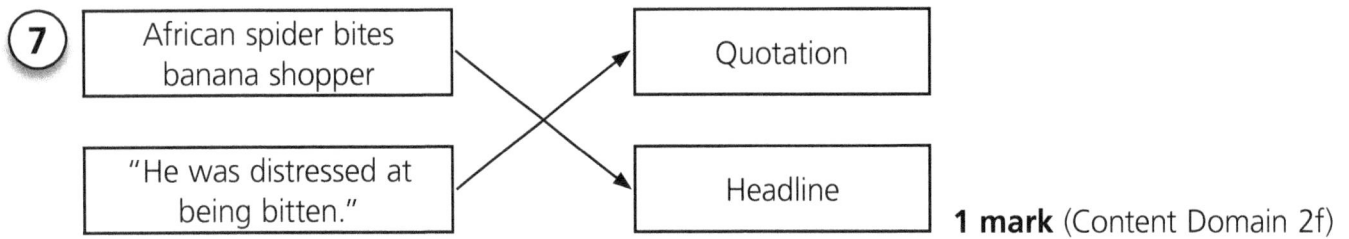

(7)

African spider bites banana shopper

"He was distressed at being bitten."

Quotation

Headline

1 mark (Content Domain 2f)

(8) Hide away to make a secret journey ✓

Get lost

Eat bananas

Hide away from predators

Hibernate

1 mark (Content Domain 2a)

(9) Pupils should write 'African spider / African spider bites banana shopper'.

You may want to remind pupils to read the title as well as the body of the text. Extra challenge is included in the question through the use of 'origins of the spider' rather than 'where it came from'.   **1 mark** (Content Domain 2f)

(10) Pupils should write 'the Brazilian wandering spider / Phoneutria fera'.

To answer this question, pupils need to read across the text. You may also want to note that 'venomous' and 'dangerous' are used in the text but not 'poisonous', which again adds greater challenge to the question.   **1 mark** (Content Domain 2b)

Roman Life in Britain

Who were the Celts?

The time before the Romans invaded Britain is known as the Iron Age (800 BCE–43 CE). The people who lived in Britain at that time were called the Celts. The Celts were divided into lots of different tribes, each with a different king or queen. Sometimes these tribes would argue and fight.

The Celts lived in small villages. Their houses were made of wattle and daub (branches and mud) and sometimes farmyard animals lived inside with them.

Who were the Romans?

Romans originally came from the city of Rome in Italy. By the time they invaded Britain in 43 CE, they ruled a large empire made up of millions of people. The Romans were led by an emperor and they had a powerful army.

Why did the Romans invade Britain?

By 43 CE, Rome had a new emperor called Claudius. Other emperors had tried to conquer Britain before, but had failed. Claudius decided to prove he was a strong leader by being the first emperor to conquer Britain.

Claudius believed that Britain was a rich country with lots of gold and silver mines. He wanted some of that wealth for the empire.

The Invasion

Claudius invaded Britain in 43 CE. He brought 40,000 troops with him. He even had war elephants.

The Roman army was very good at fighting. They were well trained and had the best weapons available. Because the Celts came from different tribes, they disagreed about what to do when the Roman invasion started. Some wanted to fight; others wanted to surrender. Celts who didn't surrender thought they would be safe in their hill forts.

Claudius's army burnt many hill forts to the ground. Four months after he arrived, Claudius claimed Britain as part of the empire.

Roman Towns

Celts lived in small villages in the countryside. Romans liked to live in towns. After the invasion, they built towns all over Britain. Roman towns were always built in the same way, with streets laid out in a grid. At the centre of the town was a market place known as the forum. The town hall, or basilica, was next to the market place.

Many Roman towns were surrounded by a wall to keep them safe. Most towns had baths where you could wash, and bigger towns had an amphitheatre where people could watch sports.

Roman Life in Britain by Ciaran Murtagh

Questions

(1) According to the text, what were the Celts' homes constructed from?

.... [1 mark]

(2) 'The Celts were divided into lots of different tribes, each with a different king or queen.'

Which of the following words has a similar meaning to 'tribe'? Circle **one.**

squad   clan   army   unit   herd   [1 mark]

(3) Where did the Romans originate from?

.... [1 mark]

(4) 'The Roman army was very good at fighting.'

How did the Roman army differ to the Celtic warriors?

....

....

[Up to 2 marks]

(5) What type of settlements did the Romans and Celts live in?

.... [1 mark]

(6) 'The Romans were led by an emperor ...'

Find and copy a phrase that shows how this was different to the Celts.

.... [1 mark]

7 Using information from the text, put a tick in the correct box to show whether each statement is **true** or **false**.

	True	False
The Romans invaded Britain in 43 BCE.		
The Celts lived in Britain during the Iron Age.		
It took the Romans four months to conquer Britain.		
The Roman Empire was made up of 40,000 people.		

[Up to 2 marks]

8 What did Claudius achieve that previous Roman Emperors had failed to do?

.... *[1 mark]*

9 Complete the sentence below.

Emperor Claudius wanted to conquer Britain because …

Tick **one.**

he thought the Celts would be easy to defeat. ☐

he enjoyed burning hill forts. ☐

he wanted to encourage the Celts to live more like the Romans. ☐

he believed there was lots of gold and silver which would make
the empire rich. ☐ *[1 mark]*

10 Draw lines to match each Roman word to its definition.

forum		market place

basilica		sports stadium

amphitheatre		town hall

[1 mark]

Teaching assessment

The focus in this extract is on *2b retrieve and record information / identify key details from fiction and non-fiction.* When retrieving, recording and identifying key information from texts, pupils should be encouraged to refer closely to what they have read. Phrases such as 'find and copy' and 'according to the text' are used in questions about this text to remind pupils to refer to what they have read and use this as evidence in their responses.

When reading this extract, pupils are also asked *to make comparisons within the text (2h).* When asking pupils to compare information within a text, you may find it helpful to remind them to focus on what they have read and to use the words from the text where possible in their answers.

1 Pupils should write either 'wattle and daub' or 'branches and mud'.

You may want to explore the use of 'constructed' rather than 'made of' in this question.

1 mark (Content Domain 2b)

2 Pupils should circle 'clan'. **1 mark** (Content Domain 2a)

3 Pupils should write 'Rome'. **1 mark** (Content Domain 2b)

4 Pupils should state that the Celts were divided. **1 mark**

Some pupils may explain that the Celts disagreed about how to tackle the Romans and that some surrendered, and some ran to their hill forts.

You may want to explore the use of the word 'warriors' in the question, ensuring that pupils know it is a synonym of soldiers / fighters.

1 additional mark

Up to 2 marks (Content Domain 2h)

5 Pupils should write 'the Romans lived in towns and the Celts lived in villages'.

1 mark (Content Domain 2h)

6 Pupils should write 'The Celts were divided into lots of different tribes, each with a different king or queen.' **1 mark** (Content Domain 2h)

(7)		True	False
The Romans invaded Britain in 43 BCE.			✓
The Celts lived in Britain during the Iron Age.		✓	
It took the Romans four months to conquer Britain.		✓	
The Roman Empire was made up of 40,000 people.			✓

The first part of this question is false as it uses BCE not CE; you may want to discuss the importance of paying attention to details such as dates and time periods when responding to questions.   **1 mark** for **three** correct or **2 marks** for **all four** correct (Content Domain 2b)

(8) Pupils should explain that Claudius managed to conquer Britain. Other emperors had tried but failed.   **1 mark** (Content Domain 2b)

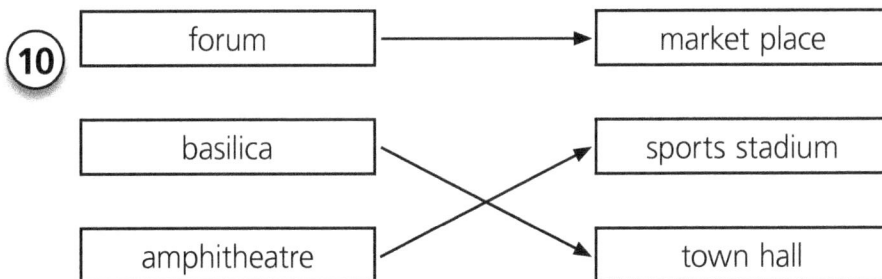

(9) he thought the Celts would be easy to defeat.   ☐

he enjoyed burning hill forts.   ☐

he wanted to encourage the Celts to live more like the Romans.   ☐

he believed there was lots of gold and silver which would make the empire rich.   ✓

1 mark (Content Domain 2b)

(10)

forum ⟶ market place

basilica ⟶ sports stadium

amphitheatre ⟶ town hall

(basilica → town hall, amphitheatre → sports stadium)

1 mark (Content Domain 2b)

The Happy Team

We've always been a happy team. We had to be when you think about it. It's the names, you see. There's me for a start, Danny Merrie. Then there's my best mate, Mark Jolley. You think that's a bit of a coincidence? You ain't heard nothing yet. Our captain's the same. Pete Smiley, he's called. That's wily Smiley to his mates, on account of his grasp of soccer tactics.

My dad says it must be something in the water. How else would you get a Merrie, a Jolley and a Smiley in one school, never mind in one team?

Mum says maybe it's the history of our area. It probably goes back to the Middle Ages or something. You know, like men in brown nightgowns and bald heads. Or plague pits. Yes, maybe our great-great-great-great grandparents were medieval comedians. Or, more likely still, village idiots!

Personally, I think it's all one big coincidence. Like the charity football competition. We couldn't believe it when the letter came round school. A local company was donating a cash prize to support junior sports. It was the answer to our prayers. It's Guppy, you see. His little sister was really ill. She was born ill, some tube inside her didn't work properly. And I don't mean sick-on-your-sheets ill, or kiss-it better ill. No, Ramila was in a bad way. Let's be honest, she was dying. We all felt sorry for Guppy. He was great, always cheerful and full of jokes. A proper Happy Team member. He adored Ramila. We thought he was weird sometimes. Most of us can't stand our little brothers and sisters. Well, who wants something round the house that's wet at both ends, screams a lot and gets all the attention? But Guppy was proud of his sister. She was brave. Brave the way a football is round.

So the moment I saw the charity soccer competition letter pinned up outside the head's office I went looking for Guppy.

'Seen this?' I asked.

Guppy took the letter and just stared at me. For a moment I thought he was going to cry. But he didn't. That would be too naff by half. His voice went really low.

'For Ramila, you mean?'

'Of course for Ramila,' I told him. 'Five hundred pounds to the winning team, it says. To be paid to a charity of their choice. Well, I can't think of a better cause than a dying kid, can you?'

'No.'

Guppy was excited. His family's been raising money for months. Ramila's only got one chance. There's this operation, but they don't do it in Britain. She'll have to go to America and it will cost a fortune. The people round our way have been amazing. All the shops have got posters with Ramila's face on them, and collecting tins. The black cabs are the same. They've got them up too. You get the odd idiot who scribbles things on the posters. You know, 'Paki' and rubbish like that, but most people are great. A sick kid's a sick kid in any language and that's all that matters. With the five hundred pounds prize money we would reach the target.

The Happy Team by Alan Gibbons

Questions

1 Why was the team named the Happy Team?

.... [1 mark]

2 Find and copy a word in the text that means 'when two or more related things occur in the same place by chance'.

.... [1 mark]

3 'My dad says it must be something in the water'.

Which description below is closest in meaning to 'something in the water'?

Tick **one.**

The water is contaminated. ☐

There are many people who have drunk the same water. ☐

There are many people or things with shared characteristics. ☐

There are many people or things that are completely different. ☐ [1 mark]

4 'Yes, maybe our great-great-great-great grandparents were medieval comedians.'

Explain how being a comedian might be connected to the boys' names.

....

....

[1 mark]

5 'It was the answer to our prayers.'

What do you think were the Happy Team's prayers? Refer to the text in your answer.

....

....

[1 mark]

(6) 'Well, who wants something round the house that's wet at both ends ...?'

What do you think the narrator means by this phrase?

....

....

[1 mark]

(7) 'She was brave. Brave the way a football is round.'

Explain this comparison in your own words.

....

....

.... [Up to 2 marks]

(8) 'Guppy took the letter and just stared at me. For a moment I thought he was going to cry. But he didn't. That would be too naff by half. His voice went really low.'

Explain how Guppy is feeling in this part of the story.

....

....

.... [Up to 2 marks]

(9) How do you think the story will develop? Refer to the text in your answer.

....

....

.... [Up to 2 marks]

(10) Find and copy the words from the text suggesting that Guppy and his family had experienced racist behaviour.

....

....

[1 mark]

Teaching assessment

The focus in this extract is on *2d make inferences from the text / explain and justify inferences with evidence from the text*. When answering inference questions about this text, pupils are asked to explain using their own words, to 'refer to the text' and also to 'find and copy'. It is worth reminding pupils to check for these key phrases so that their answers meet the demands of the marking scheme.

This extract includes one question asking pupils to *predict what might happen from details stated and implied (2e)*. In answering this question, pupils should be reminded to make plausible predictions based upon what they have read. For example, this text is called *The Happy Team* which suggests the narrative will reach a happy conclusion. Helping pupils to identify how authors imply meaning in this manner is a good way to improve their skills of prediction.

(1) Pupils should explain that three of the boys had surnames that were associated with happiness.

1 mark (Content Domain 2d)

(2) Pupils should write 'coincidence'.   **1 mark** (Content Domain 2a)

(3) The water is contaminated.   ☐

There are many people who have drunk the same water.   ☐

There are many people or things with shared characteristics.   ✓

There are many people or things that are completely different.   ☐

1 mark (Content Domain 2a)

(4) Pupils should explain that as comedians make people laugh, the surnames Merrie, Jolley and Smiley, which are associated with laughter and happiness, could be connected to being a comedian.

You may want to explain that in medieval times, people's jobs were often used as their surnames.   **1 mark** (Content Domain 2a)

(5) Pupils should infer that everyone had been hoping / praying for enough money for Guppy's sister, Ramila, to get the expensive hospital treatment she needed.

1 mark (Content Domain 2d)

(6) Pupils should explain that because babies cry and dribble a lot, and because they go to the toilet in their nappies, they are wet at both ends. **1 mark** (Content Domain 2d)

(7) Pupils should explain that a football is round because that is the way it is made. Ramila was like a football because she was made one way: brave. **1 mark**

Some pupils may further explain that just as a football can only ever be round, Ramila can only ever be brave. It's just the way it is. **1 additional mark**

Up to 2 marks (Content Domain 2d)

(8) Pupils should explain that Guppy is feeling emotional / overcome with emotion at this point in the story. **1 mark**

Some pupils may also explain that this is shown through Guppy's initial silence and the lowering of his voice when he spoke. **1 additional mark**

Up to 2 marks (Content Domain 2d)

(9) Pupils should predict that the Happy Team will enter the football competition. **1 mark**

Some pupils may also predict that the team will win the competition and the money will be used to send Ramila to America for her operation. **1 additional mark**

Up to 2 marks (Content Domain 2e)

(10) Pupils should write: *'You get the odd idiot who scribbles things on the posters. You know, "Paki" and rubbish like that'.* Accept *'You know, "Paki".'* **1 mark** (Content Domain 2d)

Birthday Presents

It was not that Omri didn't appreciate Patrick's birthday present to him. Far from it. He was really very grateful – sort of. It was, without a doubt, very kind of Patrick to give Omri anything at all, let alone a secondhand plastic Red Indian which he himself had finished with.

The trouble was, though, that Omri was getting a little fed up with small plastic figures, of which he had loads. Biscuit-tinsful, probably three or four if they were all put away at the same time, which they never were because most of the time they were scattered about in the bathroom, the loft, the kitchen, the breakfast-room, not to mention Omri's bedroom and the garden. The compost heap was full of soldiers which, over several autumns, had been raked up with the leaves by Omri's mother, who was rather careless about such things.

Omri and Patrick had spent many hours together playing with their joint collections of plastic toys. But now they'd had about enough of them, at least for the moment, and that was why, when Patrick brought his present to school on Omri's birthday, Omri was disappointed. He tried not to show it, but he was.

"Do you really like him?" asked Patrick as Omri stood silently with the Indian in his hand.

"Yes, he's fantastic," said Omri in only a slightly flattish voice. "I haven't got an Indian."

"I know."

"I haven't got any cowboys either."

"Nor have I. That's why I couldn't play anything with him."

Omri opened his mouth to say, "I won't be able to either," but, thinking that might hurt Patrick's feelings, he said nothing, put the Indian in his pocket and forgot about it.

After school there was a family tea, and all the excitement of his presents from his parents and his two older brothers. He was given his dearest wish – a skateboard complete with kick-board and cryptonic wheels from his mum and dad, and from his eldest brother, Adiel, a helmet. Gillon, his other brother, hadn't bought him anything because he had no money (his pocket-money had been stopped some time ago in connection with a very unfortunate accident involving their father's bicycle). So when Gillon's turn came to give Omri a present, Omri was very surprised when a large parcel was put before him, untidily wrapped in brown paper and string.

"What is it?"

"Have a look. I found it in the alley."

The alley was a narrow passage that ran along the bottom of the garden where the dustbins stood. The three boys used to play there sometimes, and occasionally found treasures that other – perhaps richer – neighbours had thrown away. So Omri was quite excited as he tore off the paper.

Inside was a small white metal cupboard with a mirror in the door, the kind you see over the basin in old-fashioned bathrooms.

from *The Indian in the Cupboard* by Lynne Reid Banks

(1) *'It was not that Omri didn't appreciate Patrick's birthday present to him.'*

Which of the following phrases has a similar meaning to 'didn't appreciate'?

Circle **one**.

Wasn't grateful for   Wasn't looking for   Didn't clap

    Didn't smile at   Wasn't expecting   *[1 mark]*

(2) *'… thinking that might hurt Patrick's feelings, he said nothing …'*

Which of the following has a similar meaning to 'hurt someone's feelings'?

Tick **one**.

Not saying what you think ☐

Hurting someone's fingers ☐

Hurting someone's senses ☐

Hitting or kicking someone ☐

Saying or doing something to upset someone ☐   *[1 mark]*

(3) What does Gillon's pocket money being stopped suggest about the accident with their dad's bicycle?

.... *[1 mark]*

(4) What evidence from the text suggests that Omri was untidy?

.... *[1 mark]*

(5) *'"Yes, he's fantastic," said Omri in only a slightly flattish voice.'*

What does 'flattish voice' suggest about Omri's feelings about the Indian?

.... *[1 mark]*

6 Find and copy a phrase from the second paragraph suggesting Omri had owned his plastic soldiers for a number of years.

.... *[1 mark]*

7 '... a secondhand plastic Red Indian which he himself had finished with.'

Which of Omri's other presents was secondhand?

.... *[1 mark]*

8 '... Omri was getting a little fed up with small plastic figures ...'

This phrase suggests that Omri was getting bored with plastic figures. Find and copy another phrase showing that Omri and Patrick had become bored of the figures.

.... *[1 mark]*

9 Which group of words tells you that Omri very much hoped that he would get a skateboard for his birthday?

.... *[1 mark]*

10 Omri's family could be described as ...

Tick **one**.

Really untidy ☐

Keen on biscuits ☐

Accident prone ☐

Richer than their neighbours ☐

Poorer than their neighbours ☐ *[1 mark]*

Teaching assessment

The focus in this extract is on *2d make inferences from the text / explain and justify inferences with evidence from the text.* Inference questions about this text include the key words 'suggest', 'suggests' and 'suggesting'. Pupils should recognise that when these words are used they should reference the text to justify the inferences that they make.

This extract also includes questions where pupils need to *give / explain the meaning of words in context (2a).* These questions focus on phrases rather than single words, which may increase the challenge for some pupils.

(1) Pupils should circle 'Wasn't grateful for'.　　　　**1 mark** (Content Domain 2a)

(2) Not saying what you think　　□

Hurting someone's fingers　　□

Hurting someone's senses　　□

Hitting or kicking someone　　□

Saying or doing something to upset someone　　✓　**1 mark** (Content Domain 2a)

(3) Pupils should infer that Gillon was involved in the accident with the bicycle.

1 mark (Content Domain 2d)

(4) Pupils should explain that Omri's plastic soldiers were scattered all over the place, which suggests that he was untidy.

Pupils need to understand the meaning of 'scattered' to answer this question.

1 mark (Content Domain 2d)

(5) Pupils should explain that 'flattish voice' suggests that Omri was unenthusiastic about being given the plastic Indian.

You may want to role-play talking in a 'flattish voice' to help pupils understand the emotion being conveyed.　　**1 mark** (Content Domain 2d)

(6) Pupils should find and copy the phrase 'over several autumns'.

You may want to explain to pupils that the challenge is increased in this question through the use of 'a number of years' in the place of 'several'.　　**1 mark** (Content Domain 2d)

(7) Pupils should write 'the cupboard'.

This is an inference question that relies on pupils' understanding of the word 'secondhand'. Secondhand is not used to describe the cupboard, but by reading across the text, pupils should appreciate that the fact that Gillon found the cupboard, and the information about other neighbours throwing 'treasures' away, both point to the cupboard being secondhand.

1 mark (Content Domain 2f)

(8) Pupils should find and copy 'But now they'd had about enough of them' / 'had about enough of them'.

This question demonstrates how narrative content is related and contributes to meaning as a whole through the repetition of similar information across the text. You may want to encourage pupils to replicate this technique in their own writing. **1 mark** (Content Domain 2f)

(9) Pupils should write 'dearest wish'.

You may need to discuss this less-well-known use of 'dearest' and how it points to wanting something very much. **1 mark** (Content Domain 2d)

(10) Really untidy ☐

Keen on biscuits ☐

Accident prone ☐

Richer than their neighbours ☐

Poorer than their neighbours ☑ **1 mark** (Content Domain 2d)

The Evacuee

With a label on my blazer
And a suitcase in my hand,
My gas mask slung across me,
Very frightened here I stand.

I can hear some children crying,
Others laughing, but not I,
For I'm waiting very quietly,
And feeling small and shy.

We've travelled on a chugging train,
We've travelled on a bus,
And now we're lined up in the street,
And told we musn't fuss.

And the teachers study names on lists,
And knock upon each door,
'Did you say you'd have one little girl?'
And 'Could you have one more?'

I haven't got a sister,
And I haven't got a brother,
And that is why they take me out
The first of any other.

But at tea-time Billy Brown's still there,
The twins are at his side,
They've got very dirty faces,
Where the tears have streaked and dried.

And I have the strangest feeling,
When I'm grown up, I'll remember,
This year of 1939,
The sad month of September.

And I'll think about the night-time,
When my mum was far away,
And hope that other children
Never know so long a day.

By Shirley Tomlinson

Questions

1 What was the narrator of the poem wearing?

.... [1 mark]

2 'We've travelled on a chugging train.'

Choose the best phrase to match the description of the train. Circle **one**.

slow and noisy   quick and quiet   dirty and dusty   [1 mark]

3 Find and copy a phrase that shows the children were told to behave themselves.

.... [1 mark]

4 Find and copy a phrase that tells you when the poem is set.

.... [1 mark]

5 Complete the sentence below.

The narrator was chosen because …

Tick **one**.

they were quiet and shy. ☐

they had a clean face. ☐

they were an only child. ☐

there were no other children left. ☐   [1 mark]

6 Which verse explains how the hosts were asked to take the children?

.... [1 mark]

(7) According to the poem, how many children were left unchosen at tea-time?

.... *[1 mark]*

(8) Using information from the poem, put a tick in the correct box to show whether each statement is **true** or **false**.

	True	False
The narrator wore their gas mask across their body.		
The children had travelled by train and bus.		
The narrator was laughing with the other children.		
The narrator is a twin.		

[Up to 2 marks]

(9) Which of the following would be the most suitable summary of the poem?

Tick **one**.

Leaving the city ☐

The fear and loneliness of an evacuee ☐

Memories of an evacuee ☐

How to be chosen as an evacuee ☐ *[1 mark]*

(10) What does the narrator hope that other children don't experience?

....

....

[1 mark]

Teaching assessment

The focus in this poem is on *2b retrieve and record information / identify key details from fiction and non-fiction.* When retrieving, recording and identifying key information from texts, pupils should be encouraged to refer closely to what they have read. Whilst background knowledge is always helpful for understanding a text, it is essential that pupils refer to what they have read and use this as evidence in their responses.

When discussing pupils' responses to this poem you may want to talk about the use of the key phrase 'find and copy'. Pupils need to understand that when this phrase is used they must write the words asked for and not their own interpretation of the target word or phrase.

This extract also includes questions that ask pupils to *summarise main ideas from more than one paragraph (2c).* When talking about the summarising questions, you may want to explain to pupils that summarising involves identifying the theme of a text and expressing it in their own words. You may find asking pupils to summarise each verse of the poem in their own words a useful way to practise this skill.

(**1**) Pupils should note that the narrator was wearing their blazer (and a gas mask). Accept answers where pupils have connected the later reference to teachers and so interpreted this as school uniform.   **1 mark** (Content Domain 2b)

(**2**) Pupils should circle 'slow and noisy'.   **1 mark** (Content Domain 2a)

(**3**) Pupils should write 'And told we musn't fuss'.   **1 mark** (Content Domain 2a)

(**4**) Pupils should write 'This year of 1939, The sad month of September'.

                              1 mark (Content Domain 2b)

(**5**) they were quiet and shy.   ☐

they had a clean face.   ☐

they were an only child.   ☑

there were no other children left.   ☐   **1 mark** (Content Domain 2b)

(6) Pupils should write 'verse 4'.

This is a complex question asking pupils to summarise the content of the verse. This summary is dependent upon them inferring who is being spoken to by the teachers in the verse and understanding that the word 'host' in the question refers to those people.

1 mark (Content Domain 2c)

(7) Pupils should write 'three'.

This question depends on pupils recognising that twins refers to two children.

1 mark (Content Domain 2b)

(8)

	True	False
The narrator wore their gas mask across their body.	✓	
The children had travelled by train and bus.	✓	
The narrator was laughing with the other children.		✓
The narrator is a twin.		✓

1 mark for **three** correct or **2 marks** for **all four** correct (Content Domain 2b)

(9) Leaving the city. ☐

The fear and loneliness of an evacuee ☑

Memories of an evacuee ☐

How to be chosen as an evacuee ☐ **1 mark** (Content Domain 2c)

(10) Pupils should write 'the narrator hopes that other children never have to experience such a long day'. Accept answers that refer to other children not having to be evacuees or being separated from their mothers / parents. **1 mark** (Content Domain 2b)

Swan Upping   **

The Queen's beloved swans COUNTED as 800-year-old 'swan upping' tradition begins

THE annual 800-year-old tradition of counting all of the swans owned by Queen Elizabeth, known as "swan upping", has started.

The process sees three teams — one representing the Queen and the others representing the old trade associations of the Vintners and Dyers — patrol the River Thames in south England over five days to capture, tag and release mute swans.

In February, roughly 20 swans from the Queen's Windsor flock were said to have died from bird flu. In contrast, it is thought that a significant number of new cygnets were counted on the opening day of the week-long census, which takes place during the third week of July.

Swan upping dates back to the 12th century, which was when the English crown first claimed ownership of all mute swans. At the time, the birds were considered as a delicacy that would be served at royal banquets.

However, they are now protected by law and Britons no longer eat them.

Last year's count reversed a decline in previous censuses and recorded 132 new cygnets on the River Thames.

David Barber, the Queen's Swan Marker, wore a gold-embroidered ceremonial blazer as he led his team, while they carried out their count of new cygnets.

Mr Barber said: "The law states that the Queen can own any swan swimming in open waters if she so wishes, but she mainly exercises that right on the River Thames."

He added: "Today swan upping is about conservation and education."

During the census cygnets and swans are checked to ensure that they are healthy. They are also weighed and measured, so that there is a record of their growth rate each year.

The Queen owns all of the mute swans in open water in both England and Wales, with the law being enacted in medieval times.

Every year local school children are invited to watch the annual swan upping procession as it takes place.

The Royal Family's website explains: "The swans are also given a health check and ringed with individual identification numbers by The Queen's Swan Warden. The swans are then set free again."

from *The Express* by Daniel Khalili-Tari

Questions

1 Which of the following phrases best describes 'swan upping'?

Tick **one**.

Hiding the Queen's swans ☐

Catching the Queen's swans ☐

Feeding the Queen's swans ☐

Counting the Queen's swans ☐ *[1 mark]*

2 Where does the 'swan upping' take place?

.... *[1 mark]*

3 Using information from the text, put a tick in the correct box to show whether each statement is **true** or **false**.

	True	**False**
'Swan upping' takes four days.		
The three teams represent the Queen, the Vintners and Dyers.		
Bewick, mute and black swans are included in the 'swan upping'.		
The 'swan upping' tradition is 800 years old.		

[Up to 2 marks]

4 According to the text, what did people do with swans in the 12th century?

.... *[1 mark]*

5 '… it is thought that a significant number of new cygnets were counted on the opening day of the week-long census …'

Which word is closest in meaning to 'census'?

Circle **one**.

survey   scent   temperature   celebration *[1 mark]*

46

6 Describe the jacket worn by the Queen's Swan Marker.

.... [1 mark]

7 Draw lines to match each extract to its purpose.

The Queen's beloved swans COUNTED as 800-year-old 'swan upping' tradition begins	Quotation
THE annual 800-year-old tradition of counting all of the swans owned by Queen Elizabeth, known as "swan upping", has started.	Headline
"The law states that the Queen can own any swan swimming in open waters if she so wishes, but she mainly exercises that right on the River Thames."	Sub-heading

[1 mark]

8 '… capture, tag and release mute swans.'

Find and copy another place in the text where the tagging of the swans is mentioned.

.... [1 mark]

9 How many baby swans had been recorded in the previous year's upping?

.... [1 mark]

10 Which disease is said to have affected the Queen's flock during February?

.... [1 mark]

Teaching assessment

The focus in this extract is on *2b retrieve and record information / identify key details from fiction and non-fiction.*

As this text contains concepts and words that will be unfamiliar to most pupils, you may find they have greater confidence reading the text if you establish understanding of the following words and phrases: Britons, the English crown, medieval, trade associations, vintners and dyers.

This extract also includes questions that ask pupils to *identify / explain how information / narrative content is related and contributes to meaning as a whole (2f).* Pupils are asked to answer questions where they identify narrative content such as headings and titles. You may want to encourage pupils to use these features to organise their own texts.

1 Hiding the Queen's swans ☐

Catching the Queen's swans ☐

Feeding the Queen's swans ☐

Counting the Queen's swans ✓ **1 mark** (Content Domain 2a)

2 Pupils should write that the 'swan upping' takes place on the River Thames.

1 mark (Content Domain 2b)

3

	True	False
'Swan upping' takes four days.		✓
The three teams represent the Queen, the Vintners and Dyers.	✓	
Bewick, mute and black swans are included in the 'swan upping'.		✓
The 'swan upping' tradition is 800 years old.	✓	

1 mark for **three** correct or **2 marks** for **all four** correct (Content Domain 2b)

4 Pupils should explain that people ate swans in the 12th century.

To answer this question, pupils need to connect their understanding of 'delicacy', 'served' and 'banquet' and the statement that Britons no longer eat swans. **1 mark** (Content Domain 2b)

5 Pupils should circle the word 'survey'. **1 mark** (Content Domain 2a)

6 Pupils should include 'a gold-embroidered ceremonial blazer' in their description.

This question uses a synonym for the target word 'blazer' which you may need to explore with pupils. **1 mark** (Content Domain 2b)

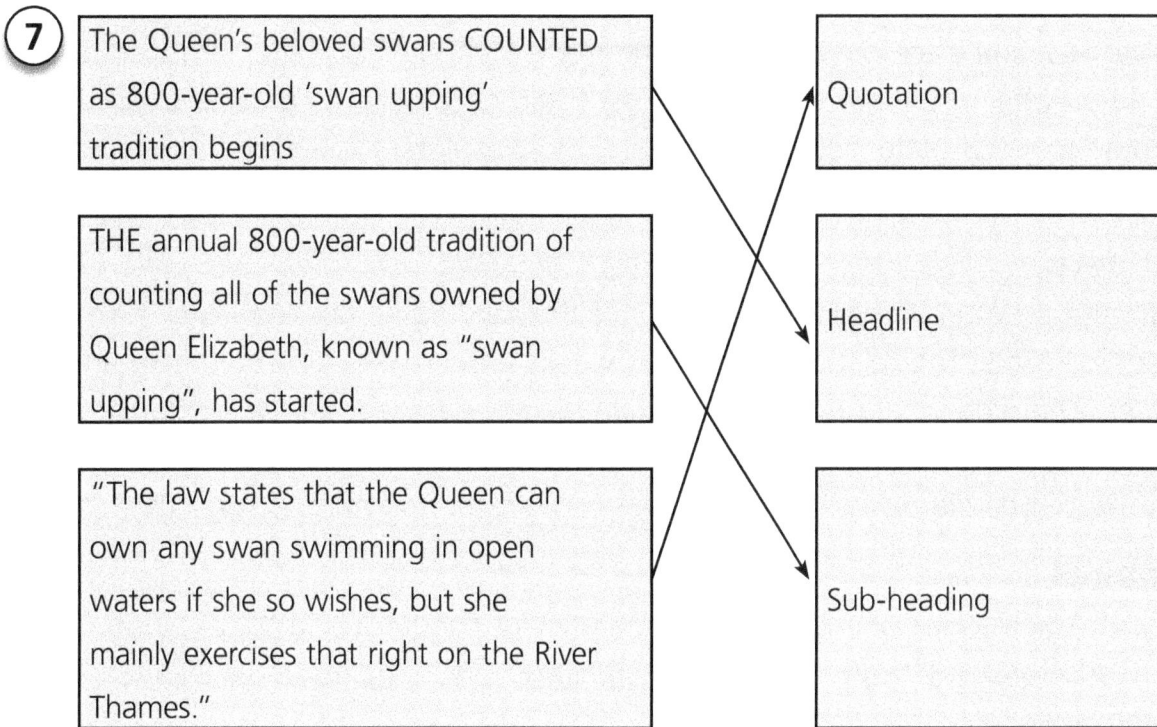

7

The Queen's beloved swans COUNTED as 800-year-old 'swan upping' tradition begins		Quotation
THE annual 800-year-old tradition of counting all of the swans owned by Queen Elizabeth, known as "swan upping", has started.		Headline
"The law states that the Queen can own any swan swimming in open waters if she so wishes, but she mainly exercises that right on the River Thames."		Sub-heading

1 mark (Content Domain 2f)

8 Pupils should write 'ringed with individual identification numbers'. **1 mark** (Content Domain 2f)

9 Pupils should write '132'.
You may want to explore the use of 'baby swans' in place of 'cygnets' in this question.

1 mark (Content Domain 2b)

10 Pupils should write 'bird flu'.

You may want to discuss the author's use of 'were said to have' in this article and how this style of reported speech is used by journalists when they don't have a quotable source for the information in their story. This could lead to an interesting discussion about factual accuracy in news reporting. **1 mark** (Content Domain 2b)

Christopher Columbus ✱✱

The Explorer who stumbled across the New World

Christopher Columbus is known as "the man who discovered America", even though he didn't really know what he had discovered!

Wind in his sails

Christopher Columbus was born in 1451 in Genoa, Italy. He was just a teenager when he was first sent to sea, and after lots of travelling he made Portugal his home. Intrigued by the spices and gold on offer in the parts of the Far East, Columbus believed that he could find a quicker sea route to reach there. So at a time when most explorers sailed east towards the Far East, Columbus came up with a plan to search for it by sailing west.

Accidental hero

After being turned down in Portugal, Columbus got the funding he needed from Spain, and in 1492, he set sail across the Atlantic Ocean. Ten weeks later, his ships spotted land and Columbus went ashore on what he thought was an island near India, calling the indigenous people "Indians" – he was actually in the Caribbean. Of course, Columbus hadn't found a shortcut to India, but he did discover the land we would come to know as America.

Age of empires

The discovery of America by Columbus started centuries of conquest and colonization that changed the world forever. However, as countries built up their empires, many indigenous people suffered.

> Columbus took three ships on the voyage – the Santa Maria, the Pinta, and the Niña.

> Columbus used the position of the stars, the Moon, and the Sun to find his way at sea.

He couldn't have done it without...

The remarkable adventures of Marco Polo (1254–1324) in China helped open up valuable trade routes to the Far East.

Columbus got the money he needed for his expedition from Spain's King Ferdinand (1452–1516) and Queen Isabella (1451–1504).

He paved the way for...

Although he died along the way, in 1519, the Portuguese explorer Ferdinand Magellan (1480–1521) led the first crew ever to sail around the world.

Another Portuguese explorer, Vasco Da Gama (c.1460–1524), was the first to sail directly from Europe to India.

from *100 People Who Made History: Meet the People Who Shaped the Modern World* by Ben Gilliland

Questions

1 *'The Explorer who stumbled across the New World'*

Why is 'stumbled' an effective word for describing Columbus's discovery of the New World?

....

....

....

[1 mark]

2 According to the text, what was available in the Far East to interest Columbus?

.... *[1 mark]*

3 What makes *'Wind in his sails'* an effective subheading?

....

....

....

[Up to 2 marks]

4 How long did Columbus's voyage to the Caribbean take?

.... *[1 mark]*

5 Using information from the text, put a tick in the correct box to show whether each statement is **true** or **false**.

	True	False
Christopher Columbus was Portuguese.		
Columbus used the stars to navigate at sea.		
Columbus took three ships on the journey – the *Santa Maria*, the *Pinta* and the *Niña*.		
Columbus first went to sea as a teenager.		

[Up to 2 marks]

6) Number the following explorers from 1 to 4 to show the order in which they were born.

The first one has been done for you.

Christopher Columbus ☐

Marco Polo ☐ 1

Ferdinand Magellan ☐

Vasco Da Gama ☐ *[1 mark]*

7) Which section would you read to discover how the world was altered by colonisation?

.... *[1 mark]*

8) Who provided the financial support needed for Columbus's voyage?

.... *[1 mark]*

9) Which explorers benefitted from Columbus's discovery? Name **two**.

1. ....

2. .... *[1 mark]*

10) Name **two** places that Christopher Columbus discovered. Use the text to help you.

1. ....

2. .... *[1 mark]*

Teaching assessment

The focus in this extract is on *2b retrieve and record information / identify key details from fiction and non-fiction.* When retrieving, recording and identifying key information from texts, pupils should be encouraged to refer closely to what they have read. A useful signpost used in one question about this text is 'according to the text'. Through practice, pupils should come to recognise that this phrase means they should refer to what they have read and use this as evidence in their responses.

This extract also includes two questions asking pupils to *identify / explain how meaning is enhanced through choice of words and phrases (2g).* In both cases, these questions ask pupils to think about the way words can be used to convey layers of meaning. You may find that discussing these questions with pupils so they hear different interpretations helps them understand that multiple meanings can be conveyed by words.

1 Pupils should explain that Christopher Columbus intended to sail westwards to the Far East. However, without planning to, he found America. That it was an unplanned discovery makes 'stumbled', which means to encounter by chance, an effective choice of word.

You may want to discuss the ethics of colonisation and how not all people would agree that Columbus 'discovered' America as it had been inhabited long before he arrived.

1 mark (Content Domain 2g)

2 Pupils should write 'spices and gold'.

You may want to talk to pupils about the language used in this question. For example, 'According to the text' directs pupils to refer to the text and the use of 'to interest' as a synonym for 'intrigued' increases the challenge.　　**1 mark** (Content Domain 2b)

3 Pupils should explain that ships in Columbus's time were powered by wind in their sails, which makes this an effective subheading.　　**1 mark**

Some pupils may explain that 'Wind in his sails' is a good subheading as it means to feel confident and Columbus was confident he could reach the Far East by sailing west.

You may find that this is a new phrase to some pupils. After explaining its meaning, you could encourage them to use it in their own sentences, e.g. *Class 6 were preparing for the cricket tournament. Amir had the wind in his sails as he was the best bowler in the class.*

1 additional mark

Up to 2 marks (Content Domain 2g)

(4) Pupils should write '10 weeks'. **1 mark** (Content Domain 2b)

(5)

	True	False
Christopher Columbus was Portuguese.		✓
Columbus used the stars to navigate at sea.	✓	
Columbus took three ships on the journey – the *Santa Maria*, the *Pinta* and the *Nina*.	✓	
Columbus first went to sea as a teenager.	✓	

1 mark for **three** correct or **2 marks** for **all four** correct (Content Domain 2b)

(6) Christopher Columbus ☐ 2

Marco Polo ☐ 1

Ferdinand Magellan ☐ 4

Vasco Da Gama ☐ 3 **1 mark** (Content Domain 2c)

(7) Pupils should write 'Age of empires'. **1 mark** (Content Domain 2c)

(8) Pupils should write 'King Ferdinand and Queen Isabella of Spain'.

The use of 'financial support' as a synonym for 'got the money he needed' increases the challenge in this question. **1 mark** (Content Domain 2b)

(9) Pupils should write 'Vasco Da Gama' and 'Ferdinand Magellan'.

You may want to discuss how 'which explorers benefitted' is used in place of 'paved the way' in this question. **1 mark** (Content Domain 2b)

(10) Pupils should write 'America' and 'the Caribbean'. **1 mark** (Content Domain 2b)

A Person is Found

Ellie had gone into the church because of her feet. This is not the best reason for entering a church, but Ellie was plump and middle-aged and her feet were hurting her. They were hurting her badly.

It was a beautiful sunny day in June and Ellie and her friend Sigrid (who was as thin as Ellie was portly) had set out early from Vienna in the little train which took them to the mountains, so that they could climb up to the top of a peak called the Dorfelspitze.

They went to the mountains on the last Sunday of every month, which was their day off, changing their aprons for dirndls and filling their rucksacks with salami sandwiches and slices of plum cake, so that when they got to the top they could admire the view without getting hungry. It was how they refreshed their souls after the hard work they did all week, cleaning and cooking and shopping and scrubbing for the professors who employed them, and who were fussy about how things were done. Ellie was the cook and Sigrid was the housemaid and they had been friends for many years.

But on this particular Sunday, Ellie was wearing new boots, which is a silly thing to do when you are going on a long excursion. They were about halfway up the mountain when they came to a flower-filled meadow and on the far side of it, standing quite by itself, a small white church with an onion dome.

Ellie stopped.

'You know, Sigrid, I think I'd like to say a prayer for my mother. I had a dream about her last night. Why don't you go on and I'll catch you up.'

Sigrid snorted.

'I told you not to wear new boots.'

But she agreed to go ahead slowly, and Ellie crossed the wooden bridge over a little stream, and went into the church.

It was a lovely church – one of those places which look as though God might be about to give a marvellous party. There was a painted ceiling full of angels and golden stars and a picture of St Ursula holding out her arms, which made Ellie's feet feel better straight away. The holy relic wasn't something worrying like a toe bone or a withered hand but a lock of the saint's hair in a glass dome decorated with pearls, and though the church stood all by itself away from the village, someone had put a bunch of fresh alpenroses in a vase at the Virgin's feet.

Ellie slipped into a pew and loosened her shoelaces. She said a prayer for her mother, who had passed on many years ago … and closed her eyes.

She only slept for a few minutes. When she awoke the church was still empty, but she thought she had been woken by a noise of some sort. She looked round carefully, but she could find nothing. Then, peering over the edge of the pew, she saw, lying on the crimson carpet at the foot of the altar steps – a parcel.

It was about the size of a vegetable marrow – quite a large one – and Ellie's first thought was that someone had left it there as a harvest offering. But harvest festivals happen in September not in June. And now, to Ellie's amazement, the marrow made a noise. A small, mewing noise …

from *The Star of Kazan* by Eva Ibbotson

Questions

1 According to the text, how does the physical appearance of Ellie and Sigrid differ?

1. Ellie was ....

2. Sigrid was .... *[1 mark]*

2 How did the clothes worn by the two friends change when they were at work and when they were at leisure?

At work they wore ....

At leisure they wore .... *[1 mark]*

3 Find and copy a phrase that suggests Ellie and Sigrid visited the mountains to maintain their emotional health.

.... *[1 mark]*

4 '... Ellie was wearing new boots, which is a silly thing to do when you are going on a long excursion.'

Which of the following is a synonym of 'excursion' as it is used in this text? Circle **one**.

pause   holiday   departure   detour   journey   *[1 mark]*

5 '... they came to a flower-filled meadow and on the far side of it, standing quite by itself, a small white church ...'

What impression does this give about the location of the church?

....

....

[Up to 2 marks]

6 Find and copy a group of words that suggests Sigrid did not initially believe Ellie's reason for visiting the church.

.... *[1 mark]*

7 *'Ellie slipped into a pew and loosened her shoelaces.'*

Explain why Ellie loosened her shoelaces.

.... [1 mark]

8 *'Then, peering over the edge of the pew, she saw, lying on the crimson carpet at the foot of the altar steps – a parcel.'*

What evidence is there earlier in the text to suggest that the church had been visited recently?

....

....

[*Up to 2 marks*]

9 What does the use of 'crimson' tell you about the carpet?

Tick **one**.

It was thick. ☐

It was a dark red colour. ☐

It was blood-stained. ☐

It was expensive. ☐

It had holes in it. ☐ [*1 mark*]

10 *'She said a prayer for her mother, who had passed on many years ago …'*

What is meant by 'passed on'?

.... [*1 mark*]

Teaching assessment

The focus in this extract is on *2d make inferences from the text / explain and justify inferences with evidence from the text*. Questions about this extract have been written to challenge pupils by using phrases such as 'what impression' and 'find and copy a group of words that suggest'. The setting for the story may be unfamiliar to pupils, so you may want to share images of the Alps, dirndls (traditional women's Alpine dresses) and mountain churches.

This extract also includes questions where pupils need to *give / explain the meaning of words in context (2a)*. To increase the challenge for pupils, an idiomatic phrase rather than a single word has been included in the questions about this text.

(1) Pupils should write that Ellie was 'portly / plump' and Sigrid was 'thin'.

1 mark (Content Domain 2h)

(2) Pupils should write that Ellie and Sigrid wore aprons at work, and dirndls (and boots) at leisure.

Challenge has been added to this question through the use of 'leisure' rather than 'day off', 'spare time' or 'Sunday'. **1 mark** (Content Domain 2h)

(3) Pupils should write 'It was how they refreshed their souls'.

You may want to ask pupils to think about other phrases that have similar meanings to 'refreshing your soul'. These could include mental / personal wellbeing, mental health, mindfulness etc. **1 mark** (Content Domain 2d)

(4) Pupils should circle 'journey'. **1 mark** (Content Domain 2a)

(5) Pupils should infer that the church was isolated. **1 mark**

Some pupils may explain that the sense of isolation was created by the church being 'on the far side of the meadow and quite by itself'. **1 additional mark**

Up to 2 marks (Content Domain 2d)

(6) Pupils should write 'Sigrid snorted' or 'I told you not to wear new boots.'

1 mark (Content Domain 2d)

7 Pupils should explain that Ellie loosened her shoelaces to relieve the pain in her feet.

1 mark (Content Domain 2d)

8 Pupils should write 'Someone had put a bunch of fresh alpenroses in a vase at the Virgin's feet'.

1 mark

Some pupils may further explain that the use of 'fresh' points toward the flowers having been placed in the church recently.

1 additional mark

Up to 2 marks (Content Domain 2d)

9 It was thick. ☐

It was a dark red colour. ✓

It was blood-stained. ☐

It was expensive. ☐

It had holes in it. ☐

1 mark (Content Domain 2a)

10 Pupils should explain that 'passed on' means that Ellie's mother had died.

You may want to remind pupils that vocabulary questions often cover their understanding of phrases as well as individual words. Some phrases, such as this one, are idiomatic which means their meaning is difficult to infer.

1 mark (Content Domain 2a)

Midwinter's Eve

'Too many!' James shouted, and slammed the door behind him.

'What?' said Will.

'Too many kids in this family, that's what. Just *too many*.' James stood fuming on the landing like a small angry locomotive, then stumped across to the window-seat and stared out at the garden. Will put aside his book and pulled up his legs to make room. 'I could hear all the yelling,' he said, chin on knees.

'Wasn't anything,' James said. 'Just stupid Barbara again. Bossing. Pick up this, don't touch that. And Mary joining in, twitter twitter twitter. You'd think this house was big enough, but there's always *people*.'

They both looked out of the window. The snow lay thin and apologetic over the world. That wide grey sweep was the lawn, with the straggling trees of the orchard still dark beyond; the white squares were the roofs of the garage, the old barn, the rabbit hutches, the chicken coops. Further back there were only the flat fields of Dawsons' Farm, dimly white-striped. All the broad sky was grey, full of more snow that refused to fall. There was no colour anywhere.

'Four days to Christmas,' Will said. 'I wish it would snow properly.'

'And your birthday tomorrow.'

'Mmm.' He had been going to say that too, but it would have been too much like a reminder. And the gift he most wished for on his birthday was something nobody could give him: it was snow, beautiful, deep, blanketing snow, and it never came. At least this year there was the grey sprinkle, better than nothing.

He said, remembering a duty: 'I haven't fed the rabbits yet. Want to come?' Booted and muffled, they clumped out through the sprawling kitchen. A full symphony orchestra was swelling out of the radio; their eldest sister Gwen was slicing onions and singing; their mother was bent broad-beamed and red-faced over an oven. 'Rabbits!' she shouted, when she caught sight of them. 'And some more hay from the farm!'

'We're going!' Will shouted back. The radio let out a sudden hideous crackle of static as he passed the table. He jumped. Mrs Stanton shrieked, 'Turn that thing DOWN.'

Outdoors, it was suddenly very quiet. Will dipped out a pail of pellets from the bin in the farm-smelling barn, which was not really a barn at all, but a long, low building with a tiled roof, once a stable. They tramped through the thin snow to the row of heavy wooden hutches, leaving dark foot-marks on the hard frozen ground.

Opening doors to fill the feed-boxes, Will paused, frowning. Normally the rabbits would be huddled sleepily in corners, only the greedy ones coming twitch-nosed forward to eat. Today they seemed restless and uneasy, rustling to and fro, banging against their wooden walls; one or two even leapt back in alarm when he opened their doors. He came to his favourite rabbit, named Chelsea, and reached in as usual to rub him affectionately behind the ears, but the animal scuffled back away from him and cringed into a corner, the pink-rimmed eyes staring up blank and terrified.

from The Dark is Rising by Susan Cooper

Questions

1 Find and copy **two** phrases suggesting the Stanton family home is crowded.

1. ....

2. ....

[Up to 2 marks]

2 '... then stumped across to the window-seat and stared ...'

What does 'stumped' tell you about how James moved to the window-seat?

.... *[1 mark]*

3 Find and copy a group of words that suggest Will had a sense of responsibility.

.... *[1 mark]*

4 'That wide grey sweep was the lawn ...'

Find and copy **two** other places where the author has referred to the greyness of the scene.

1. ....

2. ....

[1 mark]

5 'The radio let out a sudden hideous crackle of static as he passed the table.'

Describe another event in the extract where Will's presence appears to provoke unusual reactions.

.... *[1 mark]*

6 Find and copy a word that has a similar meaning to 'shouted in a loud, high-pitched voice'.

.... *[1 mark]*

7 '… *the sprawling kitchen.'*

This makes the kitchen sound large and spread out.

What other impressions do you get about the kitchen? Give **two**.

....

....

....

[Up to 2 marks]

8 Do you think the Stanton family live in the country or the city?

....

Write down **three** things from the text to support your answer.

1. ....

2. ....

3. ....   *[Up to 3 marks]*

9 *'Outdoors, it was suddenly very quiet.'*

Why do you think it seemed quiet outside? Explain your thoughts by referring to the text.

....

....

....

[Up to 3 marks]

10 *'They tramped through the thin snow to the row of heavy wooden hutches …'*

Find and copy another group of words showing that James and Will walked heavily.

.... *[1 mark]*

Teaching assessment

The focus in this extract is on *2d make inferences from the text / explain and justify inferences with evidence from the text*. When answering inference questions about this text, pupils are asked to explain using their own words, to 'refer to the text' and also to 'find and copy'. It is worth reminding pupils to check for these key phrases so that their answers meet the demands of the marking scheme.

This extract also includes questions asking pupils to *identify / explain how information / narrative content is related and contributes to meaning as a whole (2f)*. As this is a narrative text, these questions ask pupils to note how cohesion is created through the repetition of ideas across the extract. You may want to encourage pupils to copy these techniques in their own writing.

(**1**) Pupils should write 'Too many kids in this family, that's what. Just *too many.*' and 'You'd think this house was big enough, but there's always *people.*'

1 mark for each correct answer **up to 2 marks** (Content Domain 2d)

(**2**) Pupils should write that 'stumped' shows that James was stamping his feet.

1 mark (Content Domain 2d)

(**3**) Pupils should write 'He said, remembering a duty' or 'remembering a duty'.

This question requires pupils to understand that 'sense of responsibility' is a synonym for 'duty'. **1 mark** (Content Domain 2d)

(**4**) Pupils should write 'All the broad sky was grey' and 'At least this year there was the grey sprinkle'.

You may want to discuss how the repetition of grey helps to secure an image of the scene in the reader's mind. **1 mark** (Content Domain 2f)

(**5**) Pupils should describe the reaction of the rabbits, e.g. *The rabbits were restless and unsettled when Will went to feed them.*

Pupils will need to appreciate the author's use of 'normally' to signpost that the rabbits were behaving unusually. **1 mark** (Content Domain 2f)

(**6**) Pupils should write 'shrieked'. **1 mark** (Content Domain 2a)

(7) Pupils should infer that the kitchen was noisy, e.g. *It's noisy because the radio is playing and then starts to crackle. Gwen is singing and chopping onions and Mum is shouting at the boys to feed the rabbits and then to turn the radio down.*   **1 mark**

Pupils should also infer that the kitchen was hot, e.g. *It is hot in the kitchen because mum is red-faced.*   **1 mark**

Up to 2 marks (Content Domain 2d)

(8) Pupils should infer that it's most likely that the Stantons live in the country.   **1 mark**

Pupils should list any three from: there's an orchard, there's an old barn, the family have chicken coops and rabbit hutches, Dawsons' Farm is behind their house.

1 mark for **one or two** correct or **2 marks** for **three** correct

Up to 3 marks (Content Domain 2d)

(9) Pupils should explain that it seemed quiet outside because the boys could no longer hear the noise of the radio, shouting and cooking in the kitchen.   **1 mark**

Some pupils may add that outside there was just James and Will rather than all the people who were inside the house.   **1 additional mark**

Some pupils may further add that it was snowy outside, and that snow muffles sounds.

1 additional mark

Up to 3 marks (Content Domain 2d)

(10) Pupils should write 'they clumped out through the sprawling kitchen'.

1 mark (Content Domain 2f)

The Apple-Raid

Darkness came early, though not yet cold;
Stars were strung on the telegraph wires;
Street lamps spilled pools of liquid gold;
The breeze was spiced with garden fires.

That smell of burnt leaves, the early dark,
Can still excite me but not as it did
So long ago when we met in the park –
Myself, John Peters and David Kidd.

We moved out of town to the district where
The lucky and wealthy had their homes
With garages, gardens, and apples to spare
Ripely clustered in the trees' green domes.

We chose the place we meant to plunder
And climbed the wall and dropped down to
The secret dark. Apples crunched under
Our feet as we moved through the grass and dew.

The clusters on the lower boughs of the tree
Were easy to reach. We stored the fruit
In pockets and jerseys until all three
Boys were heavy with their tasty loot.

Safe on the other side of the wall
We moved back to town and munched as we went.
I wonder if David remembers at all
The little adventure, the apples' fresh scent.

Strange to think that he's fifty years old,
That tough little boy with scabs on his knees;
Stranger to think that John Peters lies cold
In an orchard in France beneath apple trees.

By Vernon Scannell

Questions

1 What time of day is it when the narrator and his friends meet?

....

Write **three** things that give you this impression.

1. ....

2. ....

3. .... [Up to 3 marks]

2 'Street lamps spilled pools of liquid gold.'

What impression does this phrase give you?

....

....

[Up to 2 marks]

3 Find and copy one word from the fourth verse that shows the narrator and his friends planned to steal the apples.

.... [1 mark]

4 In which season is the poem set?

....

What gives you this impression? Give **two** examples.

1. ....

2. .... [Up to 2 marks]

5 Which verse describes where the narrator and his friends stored the apples they had picked?

.... [1 mark]

6 Find and copy a phrase that has a similar meaning to *'we walked over fallen apples'*.

.... [1 mark]

7 *'The clusters on the lower boughs of the tree …'*

What does this suggest about the appearance of the apples?

Tick **one**.

They were ripe. ☐

They hung in groups. ☐

They were spread out. ☐

They looked like jewels. ☐ [1 mark]

8 Which of the following is a synonym of 'boughs'? Circle **one**.

branches   trunk   leaves   roots   crown   [1 mark]

9 Explain what has happened to John Peters. Refer to words and phrases in the poem that make you think this.

....

....

....

....

[Up to 3 marks]

10 Which of the following is a suitable summary of the poem?   Tick **one**.

Three boys visit an apple orchard in France. ☐

A man fondly remembers stealing apples with his friends. ☐

Three men steal apples from a garden. ☐

The best places to steal apples. ☐ [1 mark]

Teaching assessment

The focus in this extract is on *2d make inferences from the text / explain and justify inferences with evidence from the text*. A range of question formats have been used in the questions about this poem including short answers, tick-box responses and longer responses. As the poem is a rich source of imagery, pupils have been asked to answer questions using the 'what impression' sentence stem and to justify their responses with reference to the text.

This extract also includes questions that ask pupils to *summarise main ideas from more than one paragraph (2c)*. You may need to support some pupils to summarise the content of this poem as they must understand the shift in time between the events of childhood and the narrator's memory of those events as an adult.

(1) Pupils should write 'it is evening'.   **1 mark**

Pupils should write:

1. The poet refers to darkness coming early.

2. The poet mentions the stars.

3. The poet says the lamplight glows golden.

1 mark for **two or three** correct or **2 marks** for **all three** correct

Up to 3 marks (Content Domain 2d)

(2) Pupils should explain that by referring to the light as pools, the poet has evoked an image of patches of light beneath the lamps.   **1 mark**

Some pupils may further explain that for the patches of light to shine gold, the surrounding area must have been dark.   **1 additional mark**

Up to 2 marks (Content domain 2d)

(3) Pupils should write 'plunder'.   **1 mark** (Content Domain 2a)

(4) Pupils should write that the poem is set in autumn.   **1 mark**

Pupils should write any two from: the darkness came early; there was the smell of burning leaves; apples were in season.

The use of 'what gives you this impression' in this question asks pupils to visualise. This question also asks pupils to use their existing knowledge of the seasons in order to infer meaning. **1 additional mark**

Up to 2 marks (Content Domain 2d)

5 Pupils should write 'verse five'. **1 mark** (Content Domain 2c)

6 Pupils should write 'Apples crunched under our feet'. **1 mark** (Content Domain 2a)

7 They were ripe. ☐

They hung in groups. ✓

They were spread out. ☐

They looked like jewels. ☐

Some pupils may find this question tricky as it is an inference question that is dependent upon understanding of vocabulary. **1 mark** (Content Domain 2d)

8 Pupils should circle 'branches'. **1 mark** (Content Domain 2a)

9 Pupils should infer that John Peters has died and is now buried in an orchard in France. **1 mark**

Some pupils may refer to the use of 'lies cold' to indicate that his body no longer has the warmth of life and / or 'beneath apple trees' to indicate that he is buried. **1 additional mark**

Some pupils may further infer that his burial in France almost certainly indicates that he died during the 20th-century conflicts in France. **1 additional mark**

Up to 3 marks (Content Domain 2d)

10 Three boys visit an apple orchard in France. ☐

A man fondly remembers stealing apples with his friends. ✓

Three men steal apples from a garden. ☐

The best places to steal apples. ☐ **1 mark** (Content Domain 2c)

Fantastic Mr Dahl ✳✳✳

I first met Roald Dahl in a television studio in 1980. He was already very famous, though perhaps not quite as mega-famous as he is today. He'd written *James and the Giant Peach*, *Charlie and the Chocolate Factory*, *Fantastic Mr Fox* and *Danny the Champion of the World*. But now he had a new book out. And so did I. We were both appearing in the same TV programme because someone thought that we were writing similar kinds of stories. To tell the truth, I was quite excited. I was going to meet a writer whose books millions of children loved. But there was someone else with me who was even more excited than I was. This was my son Joe, who was about five years old.

In TV studios, there's often a little room away from all the cameras, where you wait until it's your turn to be filmed. It's called the green room – even though it's not usually green. Joe and I sat on one side of this particular green room and Roald Dahl was on the other. I noticed that he didn't really look at me even though I looked at him and tried to say hello. Instead, every now and then, Roald Dahl looked across at Joe. This went on for some time. After a bit, Roald caught Joe's attention and said to him in quite a stern way, 'Come here.'

Joe looked at me and I nodded. So he went over and stood in front of Roald Dahl. And, as everyone will tell you, Roald was very big – even when he was sitting down. Big legs, big body, even a big head. For a little boy, he must have seemed huge. A real giant.

Then, in a big, booming voice, Roald Dahl said to Joe, 'What's that growing on your father's face?'

Joe looked across the room at me and then back at Roald Dahl. In a small voice, he said, 'A beard?'

'Exactly!' said Roald Dahl. 'And it's disgusting!'

Joe looked unsure. Was this a joke or was it serious? He smiled, but only a little.

Roald Dahl went on, 'It's probably got this morning's breakfast in it. And last night's dinner. And old bits of rubbish, any old stuff that he's come across. You might even find a bicycle wheel in it.'

Joe looked back again at me and my beard. I could see on his face that there was a part of him that believed what he had just heard. After all, Roald Dahl hadn't asked Joe what he thought *might* be in my beard. He'd just told him in that firm, very sure voice what was actually, really and very definitely in my beard.

And that's what Roald Dahl was like. When he spoke, he did sound very, very certain – even if what he was saying was extraordinary, amazing, weird, fantastical or downright crazy.

Soon after that, Roald and I were called into the studio – me to talk about my book about a giant flea that lived in the London Underground and Roald Dahl to talk about … can you guess? *The Twits*, of course.

Fantastic Mr Dahl by Michael Rosen

Questions

1 Who is recounting the events in this biography?

.... [1 mark]

2 When do the described events take place?

.... [1 mark]

3 According to the text, why were the narrator and Roald Dahl invited to appear on the same TV programme?

.... [1 mark]

4 In what way were the narrator's and his son's feelings about meeting Roald Dahl similar?

.... [1 mark]

5 *'After a bit, Roald caught Joe's attention and said to him in quite a stern way, "Come here."'*

What does the word 'stern' suggest about the way Roald Dahl spoke to Joe?

.... [1 mark]

6 Read from *'Joe looked at me and I nodded …'* to *'"What's that growing on your father's face?"'*

How does the narrator create the impression of Roald Dahl's size?

....

....

....

....

[Up to 3 marks]

7 The narrator contrasts Joe and Roald Dahl by referring to their voices. Find and copy **two** pieces of evidence to show this.

1. ....

2. .... [*1 mark*]

8 '"A beard?"'

What effect does the question mark create in this phrase?

....

....

[*Up to 2 marks*]

9 What was the title of Roald Dahl's new book?

Tick **one**.

Fantastic Mr Fox ☐

Charlie and the Chocolate Factory ☐

The Bakerloo Flea ☐

The Twits ☐

Fantastic Mr Dahl ☐ [*1 mark*]

10 Using information from the text, put a tick in the correct box to show whether each statement is **true** or **false**.

	True	False
The narrator's son was five years old.		
The narrator and Roald Dahl sat side by side in the green room.		
Roald Dahl thought the narrator's beard was revolting.		
The narrator had old bits of rubbish in his beard.		

[*Up to 2 marks*]

Teaching assessment

The focus in this extract is on *2b retrieve and record information / identify key details from fiction and non-fiction*. When retrieving, recording and identifying key information from texts, pupils should be encouraged to refer closely to what they have read. A useful signpost used in one question about this text is 'according to the text'. Through practice, pupils should come to recognise that this phrase means they should refer to what they have read and use this as evidence in their responses.

Some questions about this text ask pupils *to make comparisons within the text (2h)*. To do this they must ensure that they locate key phrases in the text and quote these in their answers.

1 Pupils should write 'Michael Rosen'.

You may need to remind pupils to read the information given at the end of the extract as well as the body of the text.   **1 mark** (Content Domain 2b)

2 Pupils should write '1980'.   **1 mark** (Content Domain 2b)

3 Pupils should explain that they both had books out. Accept answers referring to someone thought that they were writing similar kinds of stories.   **1 mark** (Content Domain 2b)

4 Pupils should explain that both the narrator and his son were excited.

                                          1 mark (Content Domain 2h)

5 Pupils should explain that 'stern' suggests that Roald Dahl spoke in a strict manner. Accept synonyms such as hard or harsh.   **1 mark** (Content Domain 2g)

6 Pupils should explain that the narrator has repeated the word 'big' several times.   **1 mark**

Some pupils may also explain that the narrator also used 'huge', a synonym of big.

                                          1 additional mark

Some pupils may further add that the narrator refers to Roald Dahl as 'a real giant', which further suggests his largeness, and to his 'booming voice'.   **1 additional mark**

                                          Up to 3 marks (Content Domain 2g)

7 Pupils should find and copy 'booming voice' and 'small voice'.

You may need to explain to pupils that, like retrieval questions, comparison questions often use the phrase 'find and copy'.   **1 mark** (Content Domain 2h)

8 Pupils should explain that the question mark shows that Joe was asking a question. **1 mark**

Some pupils may explain that the question mark shows that Joe was uncertain that he was responding correctly to Roald Dahl's question. **1 additional mark**

Up to 2 marks (Content Domain 2g)

9 *Fantastic Mr Fox* ☐

Charlie and the Chocolate Factory ☐

The Bakerloo Flea ☐

The Twits ✓

Fantastic Mr Dahl ☐   **1 mark** (Content Domain 2b)

10

	True	False
The narrator's son was five years old.	✓	
The narrator and Roald Dahl sat side by side in the green room.		✓
Roald Dahl thought the narrator's beard was revolting.	✓	
The narrator had old bits of rubbish in his beard.		✓

1 mark for **three** correct or **2 marks** for **all four** correct (Content Domain 2b)

Greatest Ashes Moments

Cricket's fiercest rivalry

For the cricketers of England and Australia, one contest is more important than any other. The winners of matches between these countries will lift one of the oldest and most famous trophies in sport – the Ashes.

The two teams have been fierce rivals since the first English team toured Australia in 1861. The battle for the Ashes has raged over more than 300 matches. Australia and England's women cricketers have played each other since the 1930s. They now play for their own Ashes trophy.

The Ashes has created great sporting moments, heroes and villains.

The birth of the Ashes, 1882

The first great moment was actually a joke, which led to cricket's most famous trophy.

The Australian fast bowler, Fred "the Demon" Spofforth, terrified English batsmen. England's 11 players needed to score just 85 runs between them to win the test match at the Oval in 1882. Spofforth never gave up. He took 14 wickets in the match and England lost by eight runs.

The Oval test match was the first ever victory for Australia in England. *The Sporting Times* newspaper claimed that English cricket had "died at the Oval on 29th August, 1882". It joked that "the body will be cremated and the ashes taken to Australia".

Twelve days later, England captain Ivo Bligh and his team set out on the two-month sea voyage to Australia. Bligh promised he'd "try to recover those ashes". During the tour, Bligh was given a small perfume bottle with some ashes inside. This is the trophy that England and Australia play for today.

Ball of the century, 1993

Some great players burst on to the scene like cricketing superheroes. Shane Warne was an Australian Ashes hero from the first ball he bowled.

The stout, bearded Mike Gatting wouldn't have been too worried about facing Shane Warne as he stepped up to bowl. The blond leg spinner looked like he'd come straight from the beach.

Gatting heard the spinning ball fizzing as it bounced outside his legs. It landed well away from the stumps. In an instant, the ball darted back sharply. Gatting looked behind him in horror. The ball had spun past his bat and pads before hitting the stumps.

Gatting was stunned as he trudged off the field. So was everyone else who saw the ball, except perhaps Warne himself. Nothing had prepared the cricket world for his explosive impact on the Ashes.

Greatest Ashes Moments by Nick Hunter

Questions

1 Which section would you read to find out about the origins of the Ashes?

.... [1 mark]

2 '"the body will be cremated and the ashes taken to Australia".'

Which of the following is a synonym of 'cremated' as it is used in this text? Circle **one**.

burned   cooked   eaten   fried   boiled   [1 mark]

3 'The Oval test match was the first ever victory for Australia in England.'

Which phrase is closest in meaning to 'victory' as it is used in the extract? Circle **one**.

Success in a competition   Failure in a competition   A trip or holiday   [1 mark]

4 'The Sporting Times *newspaper claimed that English cricket had "died at the Oval on 29th August, 1882".'*

What do you think was meant by this? Use information from the extract in your explanation.

....

....

....

[Up to 2 marks]

5 '... Ivo Bligh and his team set out on the two-month sea voyage to Australia.'

Which word is closest in meaning to 'voyage' as it is used in the extract? Circle **one**.

race   holiday   game   adventure   journey   [1 mark]

6 'Some great players burst on to the scene like cricketing superheroes.

What does this sentence suggest about Shane Warne's arrival to Ashes cricket?

....

....

[Up to 2 marks]

7 *'The stout, bearded Mike Gatting …'*

What impression does the use of 'stout' give you about Gatting's appearance?

.... *[1 mark]*

8 Put a tick in the correct box to show whether each of the following statements is a **fact** or an **opinion**.

	Fact	Opinion
Women's Ashes games have taken place since the 1930s.		
Warne was the only person who was unsurprised when he bowled Mike Gatting out.		
The Ashes trophy is an old perfume bottle.		
Shane Warne made his first Ashes appearance in 1993.		

[Up to 2 marks]

9 *'Gatting was stunned as he trudged off the field.'*

This tells us that, as he left the field, Mike Gatting felt …

Tick **one**.

tired. ☐

shocked and disappointed by what had just happened. ☐

relieved that he wouldn't have to face Warne any longer. ☐

worried about what would happen next. ☐ *[1 mark]*

10 Number the following sentences from 1 to 5 to show them in chronological order.

One has been done for you.

Shane Warne made his Ashes debut. ☐

English cricket 'died' at the Oval. ☐

The English cricket team first toured Australia. ☐

Ivo Bligh received a perfume bottle containing ashes. ☐

English and Australian women began contesting their own Ashes. 4 *[1 mark]*

Teaching assessment

The focus in this extract is on *2d make inferences from the text / explain and justify inferences with evidence from the text.* Having wide knowledge and understanding of the world is a key aspect of inferring meaning from texts. Before asking pupils to complete questions about this text, you may want to establish their understanding of cricket and the rivalry between England and Australia. Pupils may benefit from encountering the following words and phrases before working with this text: the Ashes, batsman, bowler, leg spinner, the Oval, overs, runs, stumps, wickets. Pupils may also benefit from watching short clips of cricket matches and from seeing images of Mike Gatting and Shane Warne as they were in 1993.

This extract also includes questions that ask pupils to *summarise main ideas from more than one paragraph (2c).* Encouraging pupils to pay attention to section headings is an important part of helping them to learn the skills of summarising.

(1) Pupils should write 'The birth of the Ashes, 1882'.

You may want to discuss how 'origins' was used in the question for the target word 'birth'. This is a technique frequently used in SAT questions. **1 mark** (Content Domain 2c)

(2) Pupils should circle 'burned'. **1 mark** (Content Domain 2a)

(3) Pupils should circle 'Success in a competition'. **1 mark** (Content Domain 2a)

(4) Pupils should explain that England had never lost to Australia at home before, but that unbeaten record was now dead. **1 mark**

Some pupils may make a further observation, e.g. *It was a game England should have won and so their reputation was dead as well as their unbeaten record.*

You may want to explore the figurative nature of the claim made by *The Sporting Times* to improve pupils' understanding. An image of the phrase (written as an obituary) can be seen at https://en.wikipedia.org/wiki/The_Sporting_Times **1 additional mark**
Up to 2 marks (Content Domain 2d)

(5) Pupils should circle 'journey'. **1 mark** (Content Domain 2a)

(6) Pupils should infer that Shane Warne seemed to arrive in Ashes cricket suddenly because he burst onto the scene. Accept 'made an explosive arrival' / 'appeared without warning'. **1 mark**

Some pupils may also say that Shane Warne's arrival to the Ashes demonstrated incredible skills as the sentence refers to him being a 'cricketing superhero' e.g. *He showed extra-human abilities at cricket.* **1 additional mark**
Up to 2 marks (Content Domain 2d)

(7) Pupils should explain that because stout implies stockiness, Mike Gatting appeared stocky. You may want to explore other synonyms such as chunky, well-built and fat, establishing the effect of each on the meaning of the sentence. **1 mark** (Content Domain 2d)

(8)

	Fact	Opinion
Women's Ashes games have taken place since the 1930s.	✓	
Warne was the only person who was unsurprised when he bowled Mike Gatting out.		✓
The Ashes trophy is an old perfume bottle.	✓	
Shane Warne made his first Ashes appearance in 1993.	✓	

1 mark for **three** correct or **2 marks** for **all four** correct (Content Domain 2d)

Fact and opinion questions are an aspect of inference that can be explored in non-fiction texts. You may want to discuss with pupils how we cannot be certain that Warne was the only person who was unsurprised when he bowled Mike Gatting out. Unlike the other statements in the question, it is a matter of opinion that cannot be proven.

(9) tired. ☐

shocked and disappointed by what had just happened. ✓

relieved that he wouldn't have to face Warne any longer. ☐

worried about what would happen next. ☐

This is an inference question that asks pupils to visualise based upon their understanding of 'stunned' and 'trudged'. **1 mark** (Content Domain 2d)

(10) Shane Warne made his Ashes debut. 5

English cricket 'died' at the Oval. 2

The English cricket team first toured Australia. 1

Ivo Bligh received a perfume bottle containing ashes. 3

English and Australian women began contesting their own Ashes. 4

1 mark (Content Domain 2c)

Acknowledgements

The author and publisher are grateful to the copyright holders for permission to use quoted material. Every effort has been made to trace copyright holders and obtain their permission for the use of copyright material. The author and publisher will gladly receive information enabling them to rectify any error or omission in subsequent editions.

The Star of Kazan by Eva Ibbotson © 2004, published by Macmillan Children's Books.

'Echo and Narcissus' taken from *The Orchard Book of Greek Myths* by Geraldine McCaughrean © Geraldine McCaughrean. First published in the UK by Orchard Books, an imprint of Hachette Children's Group, Carmelite House, 50 Victoria Embankment, London, EC4Y 0DZ. Used by permission.

Littlenose's Hibernation from Littlenose Collection: *The Explorer* by John Grant. © John Grant. Published by Simon & Schuster and used by permission of the Estate of John Grant.

The Dark is Rising by Susan Cooper. © Susan Cooper. Published by Vintage Classics.

The Evacuee by Shirley Tomlinson is used by the kind permission of the author.

The Apple Raid by Vernon Scannell. © 1974 Vernon Scannell. Published by Chatto & Windus. Used by permission of The Estate of Vernon Scannell.

Fishbones Dreaming From "Up on the Roof New and Selected Poems" by Matthew Sweeney. © 2001 Matthew Sweeney. Published by Faber and Faber.

African spider bites banana shopper by Owen Bowcott. Published in The Guardian Newspaper on 11 June, 2005, © 2005. Used by permission of Guardian News & Media Limited. www.theguardian.com.

The Queen's beloved swans COUNTED as 800-year-old 'swan upping' tradition begins by Daniel Khalili-Tari © 2018. Published in The Express and used by permission of the author.

'Christopher Columbus' from 100 People Who Made History: Meet the People Who Shaped the Modern World by Ben Gilliland © 2012. Published by Dorling Kindersley. Used by permission of DK, a division of Penguin Random House.

The Indian in the Cupboard by Lynne Reid Banks. © Lynne Reid Banks. Used by permission of the author via Watson Little Ltd.

Fantastic Mr Dahl by Michael Rosen. © 2012 Michael Rosen. Published by Puffin, a division of Penguin Random House. Used by permission.

The Happy Team by Alan Gibbons. © Alan Gibbons. Used by kind permission of the author.

The Greatest Ashes Moments by Nick Hunter © 2016. Reprinted by permission of HarperCollins Publishers Ltd.

Roman Life in Britain by Ciaran Murtagh © 2016. Reprinted by permission of HarperCollins Publishers Ltd.

Published by Keen Kite Books
An imprint of HarperCollins*Publishers* Ltd
1 London Bridge Street
London
SE1 9GF

Text and design © 2019 Keen Kite Books, an imprint of HarperCollins*Publishers* Ltd

10 9 8 7 6 5 4 3 2 1

ISBN 978-0-00-832542-8

British Library Cataloguing in Publication Data
A catalogue record for this publication is available from the British Library.

Author: Rachel Clarke
Commissioning Editors: Fiona McGlade and Shelley Teasdale
Project Management: Shelley Teasdale
Editors: Fiona Watson and Shelley Teasdale
Cover Design: Sarah Duxbury
Internal Design: QBS Learning
Production: Karen Nulty